www.sergiomcgee.com

#Blessed

The inspirational & motivational life story

of

Sergio McGee

Written by. Sergio McGee

Copyright

Disclaimer

The names in this book have been changed to protect the indignity of everyone but Sergio McGee.

Book Credits

I would like to thank everyone that has helped in putting my book together. My book cover was design by Illustrated Aesthetics. My book editor Sam Wright & Allene Gunter. My author photo by Allene Gunter. My book was formatted by Serex Designs.

Dedication

My Lord & Savior Jesus Christ for making my miraculous story even possible. I am the result and proof of the power of prayer. I have a very inspirational testimony that will be told.

About Me

Sergio McGee was born and raised in Detroit, Michigan. Sergio is the oldest of four siblings. Sergio excelled in school from writing to football. While in his teens, Sergio became a professional recording artist. Sergio has written several books but #Blessed: The inspirational & motivational life story of Sergio McGee is Sergio's first book to be published. #Blessed is a memoir about Sergio's unexpected illness and his journey of recovering and healing. Sergio wanted to share his life story in hope that he would be able to be a help to others.

Forward

I have known Sergio for 28 years. We met over the phone when his cousin called my house by accident and Sergio was in the background. Sergio and I ended up talking on the phone, we became friends and eventually dated for a little. We broke up, Sergio married, had children and later divorced while. We dated again for a little while but still remained friends. Friendship was always the foundation of our relationship. In 2010 Sergio became sick and I made the decision to help with his care. Since then I have been Sergio's care-giver, advocate, and friend. Sergio recently asked me to write a forward to his book, #Blessed. I told Sergio I would write the forward, but I could not decide at first what I wanted to convey to you, the reader. So I have 3 perspectives I would like to share which are observing people in a nursing home, being a care-giver, and gratitude. Please know discussing my observation of Sergio's journey is an emotional subject for me. I have watched Sergio struggle physically, emotionally, and spiritually. Sergio was sent to a nursing home for rehabilitation after being discharged from the hospital. Over the years, my opinion of being in a nursing home has equated to a person being in prison. The days go by. People don't call or visit, you are forgotten and all the people you love move on -almost like you never existed.

Most depressing of all is that you are forgotten by those you specifically remember helping when they needed you. Over the years, I have had a lot of opportunities to talk to some of the residents and the staff at the nursing homes where Sergio was placed. I have been told stories of families driving their beloved Mother, Father, Aunt, Uncle, Husband, Sister, or Brother to the door of the nursing home, letting him or her out and then just driving away. It is not for me to judge anyone who has had to make the decision to place their loved one in a nursing facility, or how they went about it because everyone's reasons and situations are different. However, what I can speak about is my observation of the loneliness, the sadness, and the unbelievable lack of concern that people have for their family members after being placed into a nursing facility -it is gut-wrenching, angering, and disappointing.

I say to you, the reader, if you know of a friend or a family member in a nursing home to call them, visit them, ask your friend or family member if he or she needs anything and follow through, don't make empty promises. If you are asked to do something you cannot do, simply say that you can't -but that you would still like to talk to or visit. If you have seen the excited face of someone who has had an unexpected visit or phone call -just know that it is priceless and gives a person in a nursing home an instant sense of connection and meaning. Also something to keep in mind is the person you are reaching out to may not always have a warm and fuzzy reaction depending on the day, or whatever is going on with him or her. The person you are reaching out to has had a life-changing situation -he or she may be dealing with some aspect of that change, or just having a rough day like we all do sometimes -you can not and should not take it personally. Life is too short and tomorrow isn't promised to any of us, try calling or visiting another day.

The days of watching Sergio go from being in a coma, to gaining consciousness, learning how to talk, and then being able to actually have a conversation with him was an emotional rollercoaster. Sergio's good days were my good days and his bad days were my bad days. There were days his family and I were told he was doing better and then other days we were told he was not going to make it. There was a day in particular I remember standing in the hallway of the hospital when one of Sergio's doctors approached me to give me an update about how bad things really were for Sergio and I broke down and cried. I saw the same doctor the following day, but this time the doctor was with a group of interns. The doctor saw me and motioned for his group to follow him and before I knew it the doctor and his group approached me. The doctor began to repeat the exact same things he had said the day before. In my mind I was thinking, "We already talked about all of this, why is he saying this again?" I said to the doctor, "I know, we talked about this yesterday" and I walked away. I realized in that moment the doctor wanted me to react the same way I had the day before. I am not sure exactly why the doctor wanted me to cry in front of him and the interns, maybe it was to show them how he was going to deal with my sadness, or he was going to show them how he would comfort me or both.

It was an awkward moment, but I decided I needed to pull myself together emotionally and I could no longer allow the days of my life to be controlled by my emotions. I decided to prepare for the possibility of Sergio's death and also his life if he were to be discharged from the hospital. I also had to learn that no one has control when it comes to life and death, it is all up to God. However, what I could control was educating myself about Sergio's treatment. I called and spoke with doctors at other hospitals, asked questions, and I researched the types of treatment Sergio was receiving. I needed to know with all of my being everything that could be done was being done. It is very easy to get lost in the midst of a situation and neglect yourself without realizing it. As a care-giver I had to learn to take some time for myself. It is very easy to get lost in the midst of a situation and neglect yourself without realizing it. I figured out that I had to give myself permission to take a break from the situation without feeling guilty. I gave myself permission to rest, eat properly, and check-in with my family and friends. I also began meditating and studying subjects that were gratifying to me spiritually. Doing all of these things made me feel stronger and also gave me clarity in my life overall. I realized I had to take care of myself, otherwise I would not be able to help Sergio. If you are a care-giver please make sure you are taking care of yourself. The last thing I want to talk about is gratitude. I want to give thanks to God for keeping my friend Sergio alive and giving him the perseverance to never give up. I also want to thank Sergio for trusting me with his care. This experience has transformed me in many different ways. The experience made me stronger than I knew I could be, gave me a lot of insight about life and how precious life is. I learned how to not make decisions based on emotion and fear, how to deal with others while keeping what was in Sergio's best interest as the focal point, and how to fight and advocate for the rights and well-being of my dear, sweet, friend. I have so much gratitude in my heart for God, Sergio, my friends, my family and others that supported me as a care-giver. Sergio you have been a blessing in my life. Thank you for sharing your journey. Your book and words of inspiration will be a blessing to others.

With unwavering friendship and love, Allene Marie Gunter

Table of Contents

Chapter 1 'My Thirst For Knowledge'

I was born on a cold, winter morning at Henry Ford Hospital in Detroit, Michigan. My mother told me when the time came to give birth to me, she was able to walk from her home to the hospital. My parent's apartment was located just a few blocks away. My mom arrived at the hospital around 6:15 am. The doctor who was going to deliver me told my mom he had an appointment at 7 am and asked my mother if she could "hurry this up." I was born on February 1st, 1971 at 6:55 am. My mother told me I was a pretty big baby - I weighed 9 pounds, 10 ounces and I was 22 inches long. I was born two weeks later than the due date she was given. I am the only child of my parents, Louise and Leo McGee.

My mother was married at the age of 18 to my father who was 6 years her senior. My mom was 22 years old when she had me. My mother worked various jobs as a receptionist for the Highland Park Police Department and even worked as a model for a local fur coat company. My father worked at Ford Motor Company in Flat Rock, Michigan. My father began his career at Ford Motor Company on the assembly line at first, then moved on to other jobs throughout the plant.

I had a very interesting childhood to say the least. According to my mother, I started walking at the age of 8 months old. My mother told me the doctor that delivered me suggested having my legs broken and then reset because my legs were extremely bowlegged. The thought of having my legs broken was too much for my mom and she did not want that to happen, so she decided to get leg braces for me instead. My mother was told to put the braces on me every night before bed. I remember those braces being very painful. Whenever she would put the braces on my legs, I would start crying. The braces were very painful to wear, because she would have to cram my feet into the shoes that were connected to the end of the braces. The best way I can describe the feeling of having my legs in the braces would be if you had metal wrapped tightly around your legs and while wearing your shoes on the wrong feet. After wearing those braces for maybe a month, I started removing them on my own -I don't remember how I did it, but I know that I was able too. My mother told me she would come into my bedroom in the mornings and see the braces on the floor next to my bed.

My mother said she would constantly tell me 'don't take them off anymore,' but I would do it anyway. So, after a while she stopped putting the braces on me because she realized I would continue getting out of them.

My mother said I started learning at the age of 1 years old. My mother purchased some bright and glossy flashcards with letters and numbers and she would go over the flashcards with me every day. I give my mother all the credit in the world for giving me what I like to refer to now as 'my thirst for knowledge.' My mom would make words out of the letters and teach me how to sound out my words and would sometimes even write out the words. The words and letters started clicking for me. As I got older I began reading children's books, then I was on to reading comics in the newspaper. I became fascinated with reading and I discovered that reading could teach and teleport you.

Chapter 2 I Began Yelling

I couldn't get enough of reading. I devoured every book I could get my hands on. By the age of two I was able to both read and comprehend whatever I read. Then my parents moved from their apartment into a 3 bedroom condo, in Flat Rock, Michigan. The condo was near the Ford Mustang plant where my father worked. The move gave me a lot more room to play outside as there was a playscape in front of our condo. Sometimes I would play outside alone and one time in particular while outside, I was shot by something under my eye. I remember running into the house while crying, as I began telling my mother that something had hit me in my face, she peeled my hand away from my face and discovered a pellet stuck under my left eye. My mother worked to remove the pellet from under my eye. Once done she asked, 'who did this?' I answered 'I don't know,I was just outside playing and this happened.' After that incident, I stayed in the house for several days. My fear was I didn't want something like that to happen again. After a few days I mustered up the courage to go back outside, and from that experience I learned a valuable lifelong lesson -always check my surroundings. It's ironic how something can happen to you as a child and affect you for the rest of your life.

I am what most people refer to as "biracial." My mother is African-American and Caucasian and my father was Native and African-American. My birth certificate shows my race as African-American, even though I look like I am Caucasian. I remember one time while visiting my grandmother (my father's mother), my grandmother pulled out old picture albums and I began flipping through one of the albums. I came across one picture I asked my grandmother 'who is this?' as I held up the picture album so she could see it. She walked over, looked at the picture and said, 'that's you, Sergio' and I said 'really grandma?' I sat there in disbelief as I saw pictures of what appeared to be me, with curly blonde hair and blue eyes. My parents separated when I was 2 ½ years old. Like most children, I assumed their separation was somehow my fault. My mother and I ended up moving into my grandparent's home (my mother's parents). My grandparents lived in a 2 bedroom, 2 family flat on the EastSide of Detroit on Helen Street. I was already comfortable with being over there because my mother and I visited her parents a lot. Also some of my mother's siblings were still living there, so I got to spend a lot of time with some of my aunts and uncles, but I really just wanted to be back at home with my parents.

During my parents' separation, I was living in my grandparent's house and playing on their porch. My father pulled up in his Mustang, but parked in front of the house next door. I didn't see my father who then got out of his car and began calling my name. When I heard my father calling my name, I raised my head up over the banister and I saw my father walking towards my grandparent's house. I began yelling, "

Chapter 3 There Were Many Nights

Then I'm grabbed up from behind and taken into the house. I don't know who grabbed me, but I didn't see my father again for more than 10 years.

After living with my grandparents for awhile my mother decided she wanted to move. So, we ended up moving into a very small 1 bedroom apartment on the Eastside of Detroit. We only stayed there for a few months, and with the roaches, and appliance not getting fixed. We ended up moving again into a little bigger 1 bedroom apartment on the Eastside of Detroit. And after a couple of months with some of the same problems. We ended up moving again but this time into a 4 bedroom bungalow house on the Eastside of Detroit.

The red & white brick house on Lennox Street between Warren and Mack Avenue. The house had 2 bedrooms upstairs, and 2 bedrooms down. The living room and dining room were connected and with an enclosed front and back porch. Then shortly after moving into that house. My mother started dating a handsome man named Michael and not too long after he moved in. Michael was in a music band that would do covers of different funk bands like the S.O.S Band and Parliament. His 5 member band would rehearse in our basement and after a while the band started leaving their equipment in our basement. I'm assuming, so they wouldn't have to worry about loading and unloading every time they would rehearse. But there was something about Michael that didn't feel right, and at that time, I really had no reason not to like him. After a year or so, my mother became pregnant and I was happy because she seemed to be happy. Then after 9 months she came home with my new little brother, that she named Nathan. And Nathan is a spitting image of Michael. I remember the first time that I ever held Nathan I was sitting on the green couch in the living room. When my mother came into the living room and placed him into my arms. While I was holding him, I'm thinking to myself how he really looked just like Michael.

And just when I was getting used to not being the only child. She got pregnant again and had another boy. My other little brother that she named Raymond. Now he's a couple years younger than Nathan. Then not too long after that she got pregnant again but this time unfortunately, she suffered a miscarriage. She seemed to be so sad and very depressed. My mother never spoke of the miscarriage, and I never asked. She just remained sad and depressed for the longest time. Then after several years she found herself pregnant again. I remember when she told me and I seen the depression and sadness just melt away. And fortunately she was able to give birth to another healthy baby boy. My youngest brother that she named Michael.

Now my mother has 4 boys with no job and was receiving welfare and Woman's Infants and Children, that's also known as (WIC). I watched as my mother was struggling to make ends meet alone because Michael wasn't helping. There were many days that I would eat whatever WIC gave us. So, that meant a lot of powdered eggs, farina and powdered milk. And also, that big block of cheese that came in the brown cardboard box. I was very appreciative and grateful for whatever we got from WIC, but it just never seemed to be enough. There were many of nights that I went to bed while still being hungry. I told myself then if I ever had children, they would never go to bed hungry.

Chapter 4 'You're One Tough Son Of A Bitch'

One day Michael asked me to take out the trash, and I was on my way outside, but I told him that I would. But instead of grabbing the trash I just went straight outside to play. When I returned I walked straight to the trash area, that was near the stairs leading up to the second floor. As I'm reaching to grab the trash I got punched in my back. While in tremendous pain as I slowly turned and saw Michael towering over me with his sinister glaring eyes, as he punched me again. Then we began fighting and as I'm vigorously swinging he started yelling, "didn't I tell you to take out the fucking trash." I screamed 'I was about to." That fight lasted a few painful minutes, and once the fight was over, I ended up taking out the trash.

Then after returning into the house I went straight into my bedroom. Where I laid across my bed in much pain, as I just cried, and vowed to myself to never let that happen to me again. I knew that I had to do something to help get myself stronger, because I couldn't change my height.

The next morning, I crawled out of bed and I started exercising doing push-ups and sit-ups and anything that I could do to help get myself stronger. Then I went outside and I gathered a few bricks and I placed them into 2 milk crates. And I took an old broomstick and put it through the handles of the milk crates and that became my weights. I would exercise and lift those milk crates every day. And my motivation for that was to put an end to the physical abuse.

Then a few weeks later I got into it with Michael again but this time he threatened to whoop me, as he went into the basement. Then he returned with a piece of telephone cable the kind that's outside on the telephone poles. There were wooden phone company spindles in the basement. That he would use to set their equipment upon and some of those spindles would still have some cable attached. So, once I seen that cable dangling in his hand. I told him "you're not going to hit me with that", as he just stood there sarcastically smirking. Then he ordered me to go into the bathroom, but I didn't move, so he pushed me. And once in the bathroom he demanded that I pulled down my paints and when I didn't. He started yelling, 'I said pull down your damn pants,' as he swung the cable. That struck me across my leg and arm, as I tried to block his swing. Michael got 2 good hits on me before I was able to grab the other end of that cable. And as we started struggling over the cable, he just dropped his end, so I thought it was over. Until he punched me in my chest so hard that I literally flew into the tub and my back flew into the shower wall, and my back broke the soap dish and several shower tiles. I'm lying in the tub in tremendous pain and I'm screaming very loudly as I'm still swinging. While he's trying to grab and punch me some more. Then after what seemed to be forever, he just stop fighting with me and said "you're one tough son of a bitch", as he left the bathroom.

While lying in the tub in enormous pain but I also felt a sense of tremendous accomplishment. Because he wasn't able to do what he wanted, and I didn't know where my mother was, but I know that she was in the house. I never told her about the physical abuse and I know that I should've but I just find it hard to believe that she didn't know because it wasn't like he was trying to hide it.

Chapter 5 A Kidnapping

I lived on the EastSide of Detroit, but the school that I had to attend. Was in a small suburb of Grosse Point. I had to walk to and from school, and I just assumed that the other kids in school didn't like me, so I didn't socialize. I was a very smart kid and I got really good grades, but for whatever reason. The other kids in school, mostly the boys didn't like me. One day while walking home from school. A couple of boys tried to fight with me, but I was able to outrun them. I would run because my mother told me to avoid fighting at all cost, so I ran. After being chased home several times I told my mother and she was glad that I was able to outrun them, because she didn't want me to be fighting.

One day at school I went into the bathroom and as I'm urinating. I heard a few boys come into the bathroom, and I could hear them talking trash, so I knew it was the boys that had been chasing me home. Once done using the bathroom I turned to wash my hands, and while washing my hands I counted three boys, that were standing in front of me and the door, so I knew I couldn't run. So once I finished washing my hands and when I went to dry them. One of the boys stepped up in my face and started talking trash, so while he's talking, I just reached way back with my eyes closed and swung. Once I felt the contact, I opened my eyes and the boy that was in front of me was now on the floor and he's asleep. I looked over at the other two boys and they looked at their friend, and ran out of the bathroom. After that situation in the bathroom I no longer had any more problems with those boys or anyone in that school.

Once I got home, I didn't tell my mother about what happened because I already knew that she wouldn't approve of me fighting. But that incident made me feel really good because I had stood up to them.

Then one day after school as I'm asking the Principal about becoming a Safety Patrol. A guy from the local newspaper came up and asked if we could walk in front of the school again, so he could take our picture? The Principal asked and I told him that I didn't mind, so we ended up doing it again. The guy took the picture and said our picture would be in the paper the next day.

After a few days I was outside playing on the playground. When a bunch of teachers just surrounding me, so I asked, 'what's going on?' One teacher told me 'we have to take you inside immediately.' And I asked, 'why do I have to go inside now?' A teacher told me 'there has been a kidnapping threat, so we need to take you into the school now,' as they rushed me into the school. Once they got me into a classroom where several teachers surrounded me. I found out many years later that my father had seen my picture in the newspaper, and had called the school and threatened to come get me.

Chapter 6 I Don't Know

My father never came up there as far as I know, and I stayed in that classroom for several days.

After what seemed to be forever my mother finally broke up with Michael. I was so excited when I learned that he would be moving out. The day that he was to leave, I stood in the living room because I wanted to make sure that he was leaving. When he came into the living room with a bag and his guitar and as he was about to walk out of the door. I shouted, 'if I ever see you again, I will kill you,' as he turned and looked. With a devilish smirk and started laughing, as he walked out of the door.

After Michael moved out my mother met and let this Muslim woman and her children moved in. The woman seemed to be really nice. She was helping my mother with the cooking and cleaning of the house. Then one evening there was a knock at the door, so the Muslim lady answered, and when she opened the door, I was already in the living room, so I moved a little closer, so I could hear what was being said. And when I heard a police officer say that they're taking the kids away, I instantly started crying, saying I didn't want to go, and I want my mother. The Muslim lady turned to look at me and turned back around and finish talking with the police officers. I don't know what she said, but they didn't take us, so I just kept thanking her for whatever she said.

Chapter 7 I Began To Run

Then shortly after that happened the Muslim lady moved, and I don't know why she moved; I'm assuming she found herself a house. But I will always be thankful to that lady for whatever she said.

My mother started dating this guy named Bobby a tall, thin, light-skinned African American man. That also was a former Detroit Police Officer. He seemed to be a really nice guy, and after dating for only a few months. My mother decided to move in with him, witch I thought was a terrible idea, but I was conflicted because I wanted out of that house.

After moving in with Bobby everything seemed to be good. He didn't have any roaches or mice, and I never saw him hit on my mother. Bobby has a son that's close to my age, but he didn't live with him, although he would come over to spend some weekends. I do remember the one time that we fought.

Bobby worked as a security guard at a grocery store on 12th Street and Grand Boulevard. After several months of living with Bobby he somehow lost his house, so we ended up living in his car for a while. And that was really difficult for me between sleeping bathing and using the bathroom. Along with the foul-smelling stench that was in the car. So whenever he had to work that would be the time for me to use the grocery store bathroom. Where I would use the bathroom, and try to wash myself up somewhat, and I vividly remember sitting in the parking lot waiting on Bobby to complete his shift, as my mother would manufacture sandwiches. After a while Bobby finally asked his father if we could come and stay with them. Now I say them because he had two other brothers, that was living there also. The house was on the WestSide of Detroit on Chalfont Street. We stayed there for about 5 to 7 months, and I didn't mind staying there because I was able to use the bathroom and bath, as needed. I also got along with his brothers and one was close to my age.

My mother ended up finding and getting a house on the WestSide of Detroit. It was a very small, white, 2-bedroom ranch style house on Winthrop Street near Curtis. I didn't mind that the house was small or that I had to share a bedroom with my brothers. I was just glad to go from living in a car to living with someone else to getting into our own house. And with a new house that meant a new school, and when I found out that I would be attending the same school as my cousin Alicia. I was excited because me and Alicia had become really close from when I stayed with my grandparents, because she was also living there with her mother my auntie Beth. In fact, we became so close that we started telling people that were brother and sister instead of cousins, even though I look caucasuion and she's a brown-skinned African American.

I'm one year and four months older than Alicia, but we were in the same grade. Only because of my birthday being in February I had to wait until I turned five to be able to attend school. I attended Newton Elementary School on the WestSide of Detroit on Curtis Street. With my cousin/sister for the 4th grade, and Alicia was already really popular in that school, so everyone seemed to love her, but me not so much. I'm the new kid with the hand me down clothes, and cheap gym shoes. No one at school seemed to like me other than the teachers because I was a good student and I got really good grades. In my attempt to become popular with the girls in school. I started bringing candy to school even though I didn't eat candy. I brought candy in hopes the girls would ask me for some, and it took a while before it caught on, but with my sister being so popular. I became really popular just by hanging around her.

Then after graduating, I'm in the 5th grade and I had became the most popular boy in school. I was the Safety Patrol Captain, and the Student Council President, so I started dating a bunch of girls in school, and a few of the girls were friends with my sister. And me dating all of them was working for a while, but all of a sudden on a Friday at school. I heard that a few of the girls had found out about one another, and with me being the Safety Captain. Just like all of the Safeties. I got out of school at 3 pm, so I could make sure that all of the Safeties were on their post, but when school let out at 3:15 pm. Instead of me making sure that the Safety were on their post I just started walking home, and while walking home I heard some girls fussing, so I looked back and I saw a few of the girls that I'm dating chasing after me, so I began to run. While running I looked back again and I saw four more girls, so now there's eight. Then the first set of girls caught up to me about three blocks away from my street. And the girls started fussing at me, then the other set of girls caught up, and all of the girls started fussing and fighting with each other.

Chapter 8 I Would Wash My Cloths By Hand

I was shocked, as I slowly and quickly walked home. I found out later that my sister was the one that told everyone, so I asked her 'why?' I was told that she had a problem with that because some of the girls are her friends.

After school, I would walk with my sister to her house because her house was a lot closer, and I didn't want to be at home. I would spend weeks at a time at her house. And whenever I would return home either the lights or the gas would be turned off. One time when I came home and the water was turned off again, so I just felt that I had to do something. So, I waited until it got dark outside and without asking. I took some pickle buckets and I went next door and took their water hose, and filled up every bucket several times. Once in the house, I poured some water into the toilet, so it could be flushed. Then I poured some water into the tub and into the bathroom sink. I also poured some water into the kitchen sink, so we would be able to wash the dishes. We didn't have a washer or a dryer, so I pored the water into the tub, so I could wash my clothes by hand. With a small washing board in the bathtub and when done. I would hang my clothes up outside on a clothesline, but if the weather wasn't conducive. I would place my clothes on a chair in front of the oven, but if the gas was turned off. I would put my clothes on a chair and place the chair in front of the kerosene heater.

Chapter 9 I Knew Exactly Who

Whenever the lights would get turned off. We would have to burn candles throughout the house. And whenever the gas was off, I would sleep in my clothes and coat. And my mother would assemble sandwiches again. Which reminded me of living in that car, so I would get really frustrated.

One time when our gas was turned off, I went into the kitchen and started trying to figure out a way to be able to cook without a stove. After a couple of days, I ended up being able to cook with only a coffee machine. Yes, a coffee machine, and I know that sounds crazy, but I was able to cook hot dogs hamburgers and spaghetti. I would put water into the coffee maker and wait for the water to get hot. Once hot I would put some hot dogs into the coffee pot and just let the hot dogs boil. I also would take the coffee pot off of the coffee machine. And I would use the bottom plate to fry a hamburger. And this was many years before any hot plate slow cooker or crock pot was available. I know that you're probably laughing and thinking that's crazy, and I would agree but it worked. I was so embarrassed and ashamed about that for many years, but I did tell my sister. And after laughing for a while she asked, 'what made you think of that?' I just felt that it was necessary because I didn't wish to eat sandwiches anymore.'

Then a year or so later my mother and Bobby started wrestling around in the living room. And somehow, he managed to get one handcuff around her wrist and for whatever reasons she just lost it. And she ended up punching him so hard, that he literally flew over the couch. Once he got from behind the couch, he quickly took that handcuff off, and went straight into her bedroom. Where he packed himself a bag and quickly left the house. I knew that he was embarrassed because I was laughing at him the whole time. A few weeks after that happened, he moved out of the house permanently.

I believe my mother went to get child support put on my father, and I say that because shortly after. A car horn blew and she went to the door. And once she recognized that it was my father in the driveway. She loudly called my name, so I walked into the living room, as she's pointing at the door and said, 'your father is out there,' as she opened the door and walked away. I stood there in confusion for a while, then I reluctantly went out onto the porch. Once on the porch I saw my father get out of his car, and walked onto the porch. I was standing there staring at this man, that's a stranger to me. He didn't stay to long maybe thirty minutes, and I really didn't speak, as I just answered his questions. But during our conversation he never once mention that he had been looking for me or that he was worried about me. And as a kid I wanted to hear him say that. Then once he left, I went back into the house, and I asked my mother, 'why did you divorced my father?' But she wouldn't answer me, as she just walk away. And I found myself being mad at my father and I really didn't understand why.

After a few weeks he came back over. And while we were talking, he asked me if I was hungry. I told him 'sure,' so we went to get something to eat. Once seated at the restaurant, we started talking and by the time he dropped me off at home. I realized I wasn't as mad as I was before. After a few more visits I started going places with him. Then I started spending every other weekend over at his house. The first time there he introduced me to his girlfriend named Jane. And once he said her name, I knew exactly who she was, because of the little my mother had told me. She didn't like Jane and told me that she was one of the reasons why my parents weren't together anymore.

Chapter 10 As We Slowly Drove

While visiting with my father Jane would often brag about how she changed my diapers. Whenever my father would bring me over with him to visit her while still being married to my mother. I didn't like Jane and I felt that she didn't care for me because I got all of my father's attention whenever I was over.

One day my father asked, 'would you like to go on a trip?' I asked, 'where to?' He said, 'to visit my twin bother Theo, your uncle.' 'Where?' 'In Dallas, Texas.' 'I never been on an airplane before but I would like to go, so when?' 'In a few weeks, I'll just pick you up and we'll get on an airplane.' I was really exciting to be packing and when he arrived to pick me up. We drove to Detroit Metro Airport and once inside the airport. I remember looking out of those huge windows, and just staring at the massive sized airplanes. After getting our tickets I gingerly walked through and across the Jet Bridge.

Once on the plain as I followed my father to our seats, and he put my bag into an overhead bin. My seat was next to the window, so I started staring out of the window, and I was able to see the airplane wing. Then shortly after, I heard a voice over an intercom saying, 'put on your seatbelt.' And I became really nervous, as I struggled to get my seatbelt on. My father noticed and told me 'just try to relax,' as he helped secure my seatbelt. Then the engines fired up and my seat began to vibrate and rumble. I got even more nervous and excited knowing the airplane was about to take off. Once the plain started taxing down the runway. I became anxious but I'm trying to relax, as the airplane began to lift. Once we started flying the hirer the plain got the more my ears would pop. I didn't understand why, so I asked my father. And he explained how that was normal and that it would stop soon. I'm looking out of the window and everything on the ground got smaller and smaller. And I'm looking in amazement as I'm wondering how is this huge airplane able to fly and it just didn't make any sense to me at that time.

Then after a few hours we arrived at the Dallas Airport. Once off of the plain and we got our luggage. My father went somewhere inside of the airport and rented a car. Once inside we drove to our hotel and after changing our clothes he said, 'let's go see your uncle', so we drove over to my uncle Theo's house. I knew that my father had a twin brother, but I didn't know they were identical. After visiting with my uncle for a while he said, 'let's go for a ride,' so we all got into the rental, as my uncle showed us around most of Dallas. After dropping him off at home we went to get something to eat, and drove back to the hotel. After eating, my father pulled out a brochure that he got from the airport. That had a list of things to see and do while in Dallas. After reading off some of what was on the brochure he asked, 'so what do you want to do?' I told him the Safari sounded interesting. 'Well let's go', as we got into the car and drove to the African Safari.

When we arrived in front of the huge wooden gate that had a large camouflage sign that read. 'Welcome to the African Safari,' as my father signed a disclaimer and paid admission. Once agreeing to the rules, we drove through the gates. Once on the other side of the gate my father purchased some animal feed. Then while driving through the Safari I never saw fences or cages just a bunch of open land. And maybe 50 yards into the Safari a giraffe came up to the car and stuck its head all the way through to my side, as my father started hitting it on the neck while trying to make it take its head out of the car. All the while the giraffe is literally eating out of my hand. And the giraffe didn't remove its head until I didn't have any more feed. I thought that was the coolest thing. I had never saw a giraffe in person, and for it to be that close was just amazing. My father drove a little further up the dirt road where I saw a few lions that were laying in the grass near a huge shaded tree. And when I turned my head to look on the other side of the road. I saw several small brown monkeys that was just running around. Then he drove a little more up the road but then he had to stop, as some rhinos where in the middle of the road. So, he started blowing his horn trying to get the rhinos to move, but they never did. And after several minutes they finally moved over some as we slowly drove around them. I was just amazed to be seeing all of these animals in a natural-looking habitat.

Chapter 11 I Had Taught Myself

We drove through that Safari for a couple of hours. And I had the greatest time. After the Safari we went to the movies to try to escape the 105-degree temperature. I believe we watched 'Star Wars The Empire Strikes Back.' After the show it was still hot outside, so my father asked, 'do you want to go swimming?' 'I don't know how to swim but I'll get into a pool.' So, he drove around until he found a public pool.

Once in the parking lot my father said, 'go ahead,' as I got out of the car. I already had on some shorts and a t-shirt, so I just took off my t-shirt and got into the pool. Once in the pool as I'm checking my surroundings. I noticed that everyone in the pool had on a t-shirts, so I asked this kid next to me why? He told me the sun reflects off of the water and that can cause skin burn and cancer. I stayed in the pool for a few hours before I went back into the car.

The next morning it was time for us to leave, so after packing. My father drove us to the airport and after returning the rental. We got onto another airplane and headed to Fresno, California to meet up with his girlfriend Jane at her sister's house. We only stayed less than a week at her sister's house. Her sister had a pool, so to avoid them I would be in that pool every day for 8 to 10 hours at a time. I would wear water wings at first to help me float and before leaving. I had taught myself how to swim. And the most time I ever spent with Jane was on the flight back and I was very happy about that.

Chapter 12 'You're Probably Right'

Once back I thanked him for taking me on that trip. 'No problem champ did you have fun?' 'I did and I really enjoyed that Safari in Texas and learning how to swim in California.' And while dropping me off at home. The subject of child support came up. He told me that he was paying 80 dollars a week and I knew I wasn't seeing any of that money, so I started wondering where is that money going, I knew my mother was getting welfare, so where is the money going. While walking into the house I decided to ask her about the child support money. Once I confronted her about the issue she became physically upset, as she attempted to explain how she keeps a roof over my head and pays for the utilities and food. So, once she was done I politely said, 'but don't you get assistance for the rent and utilities that's off every other month. Also, you get food stamps for food, so where is the child support money going?' Once I said that she angrily walked away and I could tell that she was really frustrated. If looks could kill, I would've been dead.

Then after a few weeks she suddenly started spending some money on me. Which I found puzzling because she had never done that. And when my father came back over and I went somewhere with him, and he mention that he's finally getting a divorce from my mother. As I looked at him in shock because I had assumed that he already divorced my mother. 'Not yet but soon,' then he told me the judge will be asking me who do you wish to live with, and when he said that I knew the reason behind my mother's sudden spending.

Once inside of the house my brothers came up to me to see what I had for them. Because I always would have something for them whenever I returned. I mean even if it was meant for me because I didn't want to disappoint them.

I never had to go before a judge and give my choice. I chose to stay with my mother, and the only reason I made that chose was because of my brothers. I felt that my brothers needed me more. Then I needed the comfort that I would've felt if I chose to live with my father. I told my mother of my choice and she was more than happy to tell my father. I never told my mother the reason behind my choice. I didn't want her to know but I did tell my father. That I made my choice because of my brothers and he said, 'that was really big of you to do, and asked did you tell them?' 'No, I didn't because I don't think they would understand.' 'You're probably right, Sergio they wouldn't.' And after telling my father everything seemed to be cool.

Chapter 13 It's Like A Brotherhood

Although he did seem disappointed, he told me that he understood. Then shortly after I got no more visits or spending the weekends over his house. That really bothered me at first, but then I thought on how I hadn't seen him in more than 10 years, so my thought quickly became it was good while it lasted. Then shortly after my mother stopped spending any child support money on me.

Now around that time I had graduated from Newton Elementary. And I was sent to Winship Middle School on Curtis Street near Hubble. I remember one day while walking home from school during the winter. When three boys ran pass me so I didn't think anything of it so I continued walking. Then the three boys that ran pass me turned around and started walking towards me and I knew that something was up, so I turned around and I started walking the other way. When I saw three more boys that were clearly with them, so now I'm nervous as I turned back around and the three boys started talking smack, so I knew they wanted to fight. The boy with all the mouth stepped in front of me, so I just swung first, as the others jumped on me. While I'm fighting with six boys, and I wasn't doing to bad until I slipped onto my chest in inches of snow. But instead of punching me they tried to kick me, but with all of that snow. They were mostly kicking the snow.

Then an older friend named Phil that lived on my block saw the fight. And ran up and started throwing the boys off of me, and once done I thanked him and I began to walk home. When he told me that I need to come with him, so I followed him into his basement. Once in the basement he got on the telephone and started calling several people to come over to his house now. I asked, 'what do you need for me to do?' 'Nothing just put these on,' as he tossed me a pair of red boxing gloves. 'Why?' 'Just do it,' so I put the gloves on.

By that time everyone that he had called was in the basement. I counted six older guys and I'm told 'you're going to learn how to fight today,' 'but how?' 'You will box everyone that's down here, as he pointed around the basement. Until you've learned how to fight.' And I was really nervous as I was getting pummeled pretty bad. Then I eventually learned how to bob and weave. And by the time I boxed the last guy I wasn't being beat up so bad. I was in that basement for several hours and I didn't get home until later that evening. Once home my mother asked, 'where have you been and why is your eye black?' I didn't know that my eye was black, so I lied saying 'I was playing basketball after school and I got hit in my face and I lost track of time.'

The next day after school I fought with one of the boys that had jumped me. We fought right in the middle of Greenfield Road. And I took out a lot of my aggression out on him, as I beat him up pretty bad. That happened on a Thursday and now it was Friday. While in class everyone is talking about how there are some guys outside. So, I'm thinking the boy that I fought with had some guys come up to the school to fight me. So, once I came out of the school, I saw some of the same guys that I had boxed. Then I saw two of the boys that jumped me walking home, so I started walking towards them, and Phil yelled 'you better whoop their ass.' After demolishing the one boy that didn't run. Then I walked home with Phil and his friends. And while walking he told me 'we're a gang,' as he pointed at his friends. And I asked, 'what's a gang?' 'It's like a brotherhood we look out for one another.' Then not too long after that happened we moved again.

Chapter 14 A Few Guys Got Close

Onto the North WestSide of Detroit on Curtis Street near Lasher Road. A new house meant a new school and friends. I don't know why we moved but I know that I was tired of always moving. The blue bungalow was a bigger house with an enclosed front porch. But the new house only had two bedrooms that where upstairs. There was no lights or out let's in the living room, so I had to turn on the light in the dining room, if I wanted a little light in the living room so that made the living room really dark. I had my own bedroom with a huge closet and my brothers shared the other bedroom next to mine. My mother didn't have a bedroom and I just remembered that, as I was writing. I'm assuming that she slept on the couch in the living room.

My brother's new school Holcomb Elementary School was literally at the end of our street on Bentler Street. I had to attend Emerson Middle School on Curtis Street but across Evergreen Road. The school was several miles away, so I had to catch the school bus to and from school. The bus stop was around the corner from my house on Lasher.

While in school I really didn't socialize I kept to myself a lot. Then I started noticing that the girls in school were starting to like me, and that made the boys dislike me even more. And after a few months I was considered to be the cutest boy in school. But I didn't believe that to be true but most of the girls in school did. Then a kid named Fred got transferred to my school and most of the girls thought he was the cutes and I was cool with that.

Then one day while on my way to gym class. I had some words with a guy that lived in my neighborhood. He didn't like me anyway and I assumed because the girls did, so I went to gym class thinking it was all over. But not long after that happened I had several girls coming up to me in school telling me. There are several boys outside that want to fight with you. Once school ended I stepped outside to get onto the bus and I saw several high school guys waiting to fight with me. I started walking towards the bus when the guy that I had words with pointed me out, so now I'm running to get onto the bus. A few guys got close enough to swing on me but I made it onto the bus.

Then a week later they tried again but this time it's even more guys, so that time I had to fight my way onto the bus. And I admit that I got roughed up pretty good, but I made it onto the bus.

Chapter 15 I Am Now

Once on the bus as the kids were laughing and talking about what they just witnessed. Once home I found out that my mother's brother my uncle David had moved in. Now my uncle David is more like an older brother than an uncle, so I ended up telling him about what's been happening at school. Then he said 'so what do you want to do about that situation, Sergio?' 'I don't know what to do, but I want it to stop.' 'Then you know what you have to do then right?' 'Yeah, I have to fight with them because if I don't, this will keep happening.' 'You know it, Sergio, so when and where?' 'I'm not really sure because I don't want to fight them at school.' He suggested that I fight them off of school grounds. 'But I catch the bus home, so how?' 'What if I picked you up, but not on school grounds.' 'That might work.'

Then on Monday when I got back to school. All of the kids were teasing me about last Friday. And now it's Friday again, and just as I figured there back out there. And everyone in class was warning me not to go outside because they're going to kill me. But to everyone's surprise I went outside, and I didn't get onto the bus. Even the guys that came to fight me were looking as if I was crazy because they couldn't believe that I was walking home. As I'm walking through the playground, that's connected to the school. And once I reached and stepped through the hole in the wired fence. I stepped out onto Evergreen Road, as I'm looking for my uncle's car, but I don't see it, so I started walking down Prevost Street, that leads towards my street. While walking I looked back and I saw several guys. That were walking behind me, as I looked around for my uncle's car. Once I heard the guys running up behind me I just stopped, as I wanted to get this over with, so I turned around. The guys were maybe a few feet away and I didn't say anything. I just nervously stood there, as I'm looking to see who I will have to fight first. The guy that was talking the most trash stepped in front of me, so I just swung, and that's when we started fighting and the other guys jumped into the fight. With it being so many guys it felt like I was only fighting maybe three guys. Then after a few minutes I saw some of my neighborhood friends. And they started helping me fight so now it's six on six, as the guys I was fighting started running off.

Once done one of my friends asked was I okay?' 'I am now since y'all came.' Then I saw my uncle's car across the street. Once in the car I asked him 'what happened to you?' 'It took me longer because I picked up some of your friends.' Then about six months later my uncle moved out.

Chapter 16 While Hustling

I would walk around my neighborhood, and depending on the season. I would ask to cut grass, rack leaves or shovel snow. I just wanted to earn some money to purchase myself and my little brothers some new clothes and shoes. I became frustratedly tired of wearing the same hand-me-down clothes. I think I only had two pairs of pants and maybe three shirts, that I would continually rotate. With some cheap wholly gym shoes that I would polish to make look new.

After several months of saving money from the yard work jobs. I was really disappointed when I only had thirty dollars. So, I decided that I would use the money that I saved to buy myself some weed. So, I walked around my neighborhood until I found someone that would sell me some weed. Once I found someone, I bought the three bags for thirty dollars. Then I went into my bedroom and I poured the bags onto an album cover on my bed, as I separated the weed into five piles. Then I placed three of the piles into the baggies, and I took some saran wrap, and I made two more baggies out of the other two piles. Then I went outside to try to hustle those bags. I sold every bag within a couple of hours. I made more money in those couple hours. Then I had made several months doing yard work. And that's when I decided if I had more weed. I would be able to make even more money, so I befriended this guy. That was hustling in my neighborhood. I keep telling him that I wanted to get down, but he would tell me that I'm too young to be out here hustling. So, for several days, I kept asking and he asked me why? And I told him 'the same reason you're out here every day. I need to make some money.' Then he agreed to put me in touch with the guy that everyone seemed to hustle for. When I meet with the guy, he asked me 'what is your young ass trying to do?' 'I'm trying to make some fucking money,' as he laughed. 'I like your young ass let's talk.' After talking, he ended up giving me a 150-dollar sack and told me. 'You can keep 50 dollars for yourself, but only after selling the whole sack.'

After getting the sack, I walked around my neighborhood trying to hustle, but it was late. And it was in the middle of the week, so I didn't sell much. But after school and homework, I would go outside to hustle. Once the weekend came, I had sold out, so I went and got another 150-dollar sack. And within a week I had sold out again, so I went to get another sack. The guy told me how I'm out selling his regular hustlers. After I gave him his money for that last sack. I didn't get another sack because I wanted to get my own weed instead of hustling for someone else.

I saved 150 dollars of the money that I made. And I started asking around about someone else that sold ounces of weed. Because I didn't want to get an ounce from the guy, that I once hustled for. I thought he wouldn't do it or overcharge me, so I was told about a guy, that lived on the EastSide of Detroit. So I got a number to beep him and when he called back. I asked about getting some lettuce and was told 'come though,' as I wrote down the address. Then I paid someone to drive me over to his spot. Where I ended up buying an ounce for 100 dollars, and once back home I walked to the liquor store on Grand River and Lasher. Where I bought some small baggies and returned home.

Once in my bedroom I poured that ounce onto an album cover. And I broke down and bagged up what looked to be a gram, because I didn't have a scale. I spent 100 dollars and I bagged up 230 dollars' worth, so my profit was 130 dollars. It took a few days for the word to get around that I'm back to hustling again. I flipped that ounce several times within four months. Then I decided to get myself a quarter pound. Which is four ounces. That I got from the same guy for 450 dollars. I bagged up 960 dollars and my profit was over 500 dollars, that's not too bad. I went from making 50 dollars a sack while hustling for someone else to making even more money for myself. While out hustling I kept hearing about something called crack. One hustler told me that crack will become bigger then weed.

Chapter 17 The Word Got Around

Once he said that I just blew it off and laughed. Then after weeks of hearing about it I became interested, so I started asking around. And after a few weeks I was told about this guy, so I got a number to beep him. When he called back, I asked about 'the white horse,' and I was told to just come through, as he gave me the address. Once there he asked, 'are you working with the fucking police or are you wired?' I laughed, as I said, 'no,' and opened my jacket and shirt.

Once inside I told him that I wanted to get some crack and he asked 'how much do you need?' 'I'm not sure I just heard that it's a good hustle.' 'It is,' as he started running down the prices and amounts. Then he went into the back of the house and came back with several Ziplock bags of crack. He held up one Ziplock, 'this is an ounce.' 'How much?' '1250 dollars.' 'That's too much I'm not trying to spend that. I need something that's a lot cheaper.' Then he recommended a quarter ounce. 'How much is that?' '75 dollars,' 'okay I'll take that one.' After getting the quarter ounce. He asked, 'do you know how to cut it up for sell?' 'I have no idea,' 'okay then 'I'll show you.' After explaining and showing me everything that I needed to know and do. Once back home I went into the bathroom. Where I grabbed a razor blade, then went into my bedroom. Then I took the quarter ounce and I poured it onto an album cover. And I took the razor and started cutting the chunk of crack. But I didn't have any bags that size, so I used some weed baggies. Once done I had 220 dollars' worth of dime rocks.

When I went back to hustling, I had weed and crack. The word got around that I'm hustlin both. And the crack started selling like crazy. I would be sold out within a few days. I was the only person that I knew of in my neighborhood that was selling both, and after a few months. Some of the other hustlers were selling crack also, and things started slowing down, so I decided to get myself a job. I was trying to offset the money that I wasn't making hustling. When an older caucasian guy named Charles, that lived down the street. And he worked for himself installing shower tiles in new homes.

Chapter 18 Into 2 Ten Gallon Buckets

While dribbling a basketball in the middle of the street. I saw Charles' pickup truck driving up the street towards me. So, I started waving my hands and Charles pulled over and stopped. Once he pulled over, I asked, 'do you need any help?' 'I could always use good help, Sergio,' as we started talking. Then Charles offered me a job to work with him. Then I asked, 'what about my friend Stan?' 'The kid that lives next door to me?' 'Yeah' 'sure you guys just be in front of my house in the morning at 8 am ready to work.' 'Okay,' as I dribbled down the street to Stan's house. When he came to the door, I told him that Charles said that we can work with him in the morning, but we need to be ready in front of his house at 8 am in the morning. 'That's great I'll be there.'

The next morning me and Stan was outside waiting for Charles to come outside. Once Charles came out of the house. He saw me and Stan ready and waiting as we all got into his pickup and drove to what I believe was Utica, Michigan. Where the new house was being built. Once at the site of the new house. Charles explained what he wanted us to do, so me and Stan started mixing up mud for Charles. That he would use to put the shower tiles onto the walls. We would put the mud that we mixed. Into 2 ten gallon buckets then carry those buckets up onto 2 by 4 boards to the second floor, because there were no stairs.

Chapter 19 I Had To Do Something

Charles would pay every week with a personal check. That had to be cashed at his bank, but I didn't have anykind of identification. Other then a School ID, so I couldn't go to the bank. I found a liquor store on 8 mile Road to cash my check. That would charge a dollar for every hundred dollars that was on my check. And I didn't have a problem with that because they would've charged that if I had identification.

That job was seasonal, so I would hustle and work. I've always been a fan of certain money. And unlike hustling where money wasn't certain. There were plenty of times that I would use money from my check to buy more drugs. I wasn't making enough money by just hustling. And I don't think that my mother knew I was hustling. I'm assumed she thought I was still getting money from doing yard work.

Some weeks of hustling would be really good, and I would make money. But other weeks would be really slow, and I wouldn't make anything. I had to do something in hopes of generating more clientele, so I decided to make my weed baggies a lot thicker, in hopes of drumming up more clientele. The crack that I was hustling was good, and I knew that because I would have a crack head test out the crack. And depending on what he said I would or wouldn't buy.

Chapter 20 The Weekend

An older Africa American man named Mike. That I would have text out the crack. While testing the product we would always have very interesting conversations. He would tell me about how many years ago. He was the notorious drug dealer of our neighborhood. And I would always ask him different questions about hustling, and he would give me his perspective, and I could tell that he once hustled. The knowledge that he had about the hustling game was priceless. He would always tell me 'I like talking with you because you listen. Unlike these fools out here hustling I just wanted to tell them not to make some of the mistakes that I made'. A lot of the hustling game that I developed in the beginning. I got from my conversation with Mike.

Then one day while testing some product I asked him 'what happened?' He told me I was the only person to ever ask him that. He told me that he was getting money. When he hooked up with this female, and they started dating. And he would have her hold money for him and one day when he came through to get the money she was gone with his 10 grand. Then he found out later that she was sleeping with his boy, and how they had set him up, so with no money and being depressed. He broke the golden rule of hustling, and got high on his own supply. 'Within a year I became a fucking crack head, so whatever you do. Always have a second and third back up plane, because this hustling shit doesn't last'.

I left there having a better appreciation for Mike. While knowing that I had to make some planes. I went into the house and I called my uncle Lamar. About a job that he said would be available soon. While talking I asked about spending the weekend over his house. He told me that I could, so that Friday he came to pick me up, and I was only post to stay the weekend, but I ended up staying the whole summer. My uncle would always leave some money and a note on the kitchen table before leaving for work. That would read get me some brownie mix and y'all keep the change, and don't fuck up my house'. Me and my cozen Mark my uncle youngest son, would go get the brownie mix, and return to the house to have some fun.

Chapter 21 'We Need To Go Right Now'

Mark recommended that we should do something different today. So, I asked, 'like what?' He went and got his high school yearbook. And told me to pick out any girl that's in that book and he'll call her over, as he handed me the book. 'Any girl?' 'Any girl.' So, I took the book and started looking through the book. Then I picked a picture and I showed it to him. He took the book and went to go get his little black book and the telephone. Then he called the girl and I couldn't believe it I could've picked anyone, but he had her number, as I sat there amazed. He asked her to come over and to bring a friend. Then he told me 'they'll be over within an hour,' so we went to change our clothes.

About an hour later Mark opened the door and the girls walked into the house. While talking and laughing in the family room. I eventually went into the back bedroom with the girl that I picked. And after making out with the girl. I went back into the family room but I didn't see Mark. I just assumed that he was in his bedroom with the other girl. Mark is a pretty boy, so he would have girls come over every other day.

I really had a good time that summer. I was still at my uncle's house when he received a telephone call, that my grandfather (his father) had been rushed to the hospital. Mark wasn't home at the time, so my uncle said, 'we need to go right now,' as we got into his pickup truck..

Chapter 22 It's Going To Be Okay'

Once in the truck I asked, 'what's wrong?' He told me with tears in his eyes, that his father had been rushed to the hospital. My uncle lived in Romulus, Michigan at that time, but the hospital was located in Southfield, Michigan. And for those that may not know, that's a good 40-minute drive but my uncle got there in about 10 minutes.

Once we arrived pretty much my whole family was there already, and a couple of my aunties are nurses. So, after waiting for a while a doctor came into the waiting area and asked, 'who's family?' 'We all are,' as the doctor started explaining what was going on with my grandfather. But he was using medical language that I didn't understand, so that's when my aunties said, 'we're nurses.' So, the doctor started explaining his condition to them and once done. The doctor left and my aunties translated what he said to the rest of the family. I just remember them saying that he had a savior tumor on his brain and that he needed surgery immediately.

The hospital performed the surgery, and everything seemed to go well. I remember visiting with him the next day with my mother. And she brought him some Ox Tale Soup and cornbread. And while he was eating, we were watching a Michigan Panthers football game on television. He was very alert talking and laughing. My grandfather would call me cereal instead of Sergio, as a joke. A nurse came into the room to give him some medication, and told him how he needed to cover himself up, as she walked away. I saw that he was struggling to cover himself, so I got up and helped. I stayed a little longer, then I told him, 'I love you and I'll be back up tomorrow.' 'Okay cereal,' as we laughed.

The next day I'm told by my mother that my grandfather had passed. I couldn't believe that with tears in my eyes while saying 'I was just up there with him talking and laughing.' So, my family ended back up at the hospital, and were in the waiting area once again. As everyone was crying, I left out and found a bathroom that was down the hall. Once in there I started crying loudly and, in my anger, I punched the mirror and grabbed the sink. While crying my uncle Lamar walked into the bathroom and put his arm around me. While saying 'it's going to be okay,' as we walked back into the waiting area. Where everyone was wondering who signed for the surgery. And for whatever reason most people assumed that my uncle Lamar signed. Only to find out that the hospital performed the surgery with only an X instead of a signature. That my grandfather supposedly wrote himself. Once home I found myself thinking about all of the talks that we've had over the years.

Chapter 23 I Started Thinking About

The more I thought about him the more I cried. I remembered him telling me how he met my grandmother. And why they ended up living in Detroit, Michigan. He also told me why at that time my grandmother was living in California and my grandfather was here in Detroit. He would tell me 'I know it sounds crazy with me being here and your grandmother being in California, but always remember it's not her fault.'

I was still saddened with the passing of my grandfather, but I also haven't found a new school for me to attend. Since being kicked out of Emerson Middle School for gang fighting. So, I called my cousin/sister Alicia and I told her about my problem. And she suggested that I attend her school, so I asked how? She told me to just go up to her school and enroll and use her address.

So, the next day I walked several miles to Taft Middle School on Burt Road. Once in the school I was able to enroll myself within two days. I was really excited to be enrolled into school again and was readily looking forward to attending school with my sister again. Once school started, I ended up staying with her again because she only lived a few blocks away from the school on 7-mile Road. When I first started attending that school everything seemed to be going really well. I had gym class with my sister and just like at Newton. I became really popular because of her. And once the girls in school started liking me the boys didn't and I really never understood that. I finished the 7th grade and now I'm going to the 8th grade. And that was the year the school had started an 8th-grade basketball tournament. When I learned about the tournament. I became really excited because I love playing and I'm pretty good, but I didn't have any high top gym shoes to play. So, I called my auntie Dana and I told her about not having gym shoes to play, so a few days later. She brought me over some real Nike high top gym shoes with a headband and matching wristbands. I was excited to have what I needed to be able to play.

The very first team that I had to play against was my sister's class. There were boys and girls on the team's, but mostly boys. And my sister was the only girl on her team, but don't get it twisted she could hoop better than most of them. I didn't want to check my sister because she's my sister. So during the game I wasn't playing like I'm capable of playing but she was playing to win. And I'll never forget what she told me while running up the court. 'You better start playing to win punk,' as I laughed it off. Then I started thinking about what she said and the more I thought about it the more it made since. So, I started playing my game like she wasn't on the other team.

My team ended up wining the game and I scored over 20 points. I knew my sister wanted me to play my best, so she could beat me. Then after the game she told me 'you only scored like that because I wasn't checking you,' as I laughed and said 'I would've scored even more if you were checking me.' My class ended up winning the basketball championship, and I was named the most valuable player.

My gym Teacher Mr. Mosley told me that he needed to speak with me about my future. He told me to meet him at his office on Monday morning. So, on Monday morning I arrived at his office and he came right out and asked.

Chapter 24 I Gave Them All

'What high school are you thinking about attending?' 'I really hadn't thought about that, but why do you ask?' 'I know a coach at a private high school that wants to meet with you. I've already told him about you being a good student and a great athlete. I would like for you to meet with him and just see if you like what he has to say.' 'I'll meet with him but when?' 'The coach will be calling you after the school year. I gave him your phone number already.' 'Okay that's fine.'

And later that year the school was having an 8th grade Senior field trip to Cedar Point. The school had rented several charter busses, and I had never been to Cedar Point before, so I was excited about going. All of the 8th graders were loading onto the busses. And when I got onto the bus, I ended up sitting next to this girl that a lot of the boys seemed to like. And during the 2 1/2 hour ride the girl fell asleep, and her head was on my shoulder. Then her head slipped off of my shoulder and landed near my lap. And everyone near me thought I was getting a blow job, as I explained that I wasn't.

Then once at Cedar Point, I got off of the bus and I started looking for my sister. Once I found her and she was with some of her girlfriends, so I decided that I would hang out with them. After walking around the park for a while. I saw some games that I wanted to play, so I told them I'll catch up with them later. As I walked over towards the game that caught my attention. Which was a basketball game that I had to shoot the basketball into the basketball rim to win a prize. So, I started playing the game and I started winning and I ended up winning five of the big prizes and several of the smaller ones. And after winning my 5th big prize. The guy operating the game told me that I can no longer play that game. So, I asked, 'why?' I was told because I've won too much, so I grabbed my stuffed animals and I started walking around the park. When I saw my sister and her friends, I asked them to help me hold some of the stuff animals.

After walking around a little more I found another game area that included that same basketball game. So, I went over there and started playing and after winning several big and small prizes. The same thing happen, as I was told that I could no longer play, so I just stood there next to my prizes. When I saw my sister and her friends walking by. I asked them to help me carry the stuffed animals. I had won over thirty stuffed animals. And once on the bus I gave all of them to my sister.

Now it's graduation time and the ceremony was being held at Henry Ford High School on Evergreen Road. Once inside of the auditorium as I'm looking pretty sharp in my Miami Vice style outfit that my auntie Dana bought. Then I saw one of my teachers and she stopped and asked me to say a few words at the beginning of the ceremony. 'Why me?' 'You're really popular, Sergio, so you'll be fine, and you got 15 minutes,' as she walked away saying 'thank you.' I wasn't able to write anything down so I just went up there and spoke for about ten minutes. The crowed clapped once I was done, as I expected.

Once I graduated my school records were automatically sent to Henry Ford High School. Because I used my sister's address to attend Taft Middle School, so that was the school you're sent to. But I'm living with my mother on Curtis Street now, so I'm able to attend RedFord High School which is a lot closer. And after several weeks I got a telephone call from a man that introduced himself to me as Coach Redden. He told me that he's the Head Basketball Coach of Catholic Center High School. 'I spoke with your Middle School Coach Mosley about calling.

Chapter 25 I Was Really Impressed

He asked if I ever heard of Catholic Center? 'No, I haven't.' 'I'm surprised that you never heard of the school. Now would you have a problem with it being a Catholic School?' 'I don't think so.' And after speaking with him for a while. He invited me to come up to visit the school, as I'm given a date address and time.

Once off of the telephone when the time came I gave my auntie Dana a call and I ask for a ride up to the school tomorrow. 'What time'? I told her I needed to be there at 7:30 am, 'Okay I'll take you .' And she arrived in front of my house around 7:15 am. I walked out of the house in an Adidas tracksuit with matching top ten gym shoes, and a long tail of hair. After giving her the address, we drove to the school. I arrived at the school around 7:25 am. And once out of the car I looked around and I couldn't believe how beautiful the school looked with its manicured landscaping.

Then once inside as I'm walking, I was amazed by how large and clean everything was. I saw a few caucasian girls in the hallways which I expected with the school being located in the suburbs. The coach that I spoke with on the telephone walked up to me, as he extended his hand while saying 'you must be Sergio' 'I am,' as we shook hands. He introduced himself again as Coach Redden, then said, 'follow me,' as we started walking. And while walking through the school he started telling me about the history of the school. Then he asked, 'what do you think about our school so far?' 'It looks beautiful,' as we're walking I saw a Priest and he must have notice, as he said, 'he's a teacher here.' 'That makes sense this is a Catholic School,' as we continued walking. Then he opened up some double doors and I'm shown their gym and it was massive like a college size gym. When I stepped into the gym, he pushed a button on the wall and the bleachers came out of the wall. I had never seen anything like that before and we walked around the corner. Where he showed me their weight room and I saw equipment that I had never seen before. Then we walked a little more and he showed me their massive cafeteria. With countless tables and several vending machines. Then he said, 'let's go into my office,' as we walked over to the other side of the school into his very large office.

Once inside he said, 'have a seat,' as I sat and he sat behind his desk. Then he expressed that he really wanted me to play basketball for Catholic Center and asked, 'so what do you think?' 'I'm really impressed with everything that I've seen but I would need to think about this.' He said he understood and mentioned that school started in a few weeks, so he would need my decision soon. Once done we shook hands and he offered to show me out but I told him 'no need I know my way out,' as I walked out of his office and through the school. Once back inside of my aunties car she asked, 'so how did it go?' 'I was really impressed with what I seen,' as she drove me back home.

Chapter 26 'You Don't Know'

After a week Coach Redden called and asked, 'have you made a decision yet?' 'Not really but I'm leaning towards Catholic Center.' 'That's great'! Then I asked, 'how much is tuition there?' 'About 25 thousand,' as I paused at the enormous amount. 'I know that's a lot of money but I could help you with that cost if you choice CC.' 'How'? 'I will get them to reduce thousands from your tuition if you choose CC.' 'I would have to speak about this with my father because he would be the one paying.' 'That's fine but you need to speak with him soon because school starts in two weeks.'

Once off the telephone I called my father and I told him all about my visit and the cost. 'That's a lot of money, Sergio' 'I know' then I told him what the coach said about reducing the cost. 'If he can get the reduction then I'll pay the money, but only if.' I thanked my father before hanging up the telephone. Then I beeped the coach and when he called back. I told him what my father said, 'that's great news, Sergio in fact I'm going to let you go so I can get that done right now. So, make sure that you're here at 7:30 am on Monday morning?' 'I'll be there.'

Then I called and spoke with my auntie Dana about getting a ride to school in the morning. 'Okay I'll be able to take you throughout the week but I won't be able to pick you up, so you may have to catch the bus home.' 'That's fine I'm just thankful to be getting a ride every day.' 'So, what time do you have to be at school?' '7:30 am.' 'Okay that's good I have to drop off your cousin at school in the morning, so I'll be at your house around 6:30 am,' as I thanked her.

I would wake up about 4:45 am to take my shower and get dressed in my clothes that I had laid out the night before. I wore my Levi jeans and matching jacket. A blue and red Adidas T-shirt with some red white and blue Adidas top ten gym shoes.

My auntie arrived at my house around 6:30 am. Once I got into the car, I spoke to everyone, but my cousin Tina didn't speak. She just looked back and gave me a real evil look and turned back around. I assumed that she was upset because she had to wake up earlier. My auntie would drop off my cousin Tina at school first. Then we would drive by RedFord High School on our way to Catholic Center. I would arrive at school around 7:15 am and every day before class I had to attend Mass at a church that was inside of the school.

I was nervous while attending Mass because I hadn't been inside of a church in many years. After the service, as I'm walking out a Priest pulled me to the side. And he started telling me how I can't wear what I had on and how I need to be in dress paints a collar shirt. With a sweater and dress shoes and he also told me that I needed to cut my hair 'it's too long in the back.'

Once in my homeroom class my teacher Mr. Fletcher which is also the Defensive Head Football Coach. Also said the same things that the Priest had mentioned.

So, after catching the bus home I told my mother what I was told at school and she said, 'I can't afford to buy you new clothes you better call your father.' So, I called my father and after explaining the situation he told me that he would get everything that I need for school that weekend. Then I called my auntie Dana and I told her that I needed to get my hair cut shorter. Now my reason for calling her was because she's a professional hair stylist. And when she agreed to cut my hair, I walked a few miles to her house, and she cut my hair in her kitchen.

On Monday morning I had everything that I needed. And after my shower and getting dressed in the new clothes. I really didn't like how I looked or felt. I looked as if I was dressed for church and I didn't like my hair being short. Once at school and after Mass. The same Priest pulled me to the side and said, 'now that's how you should be dressed, and nice haircut,' as I walked away. I started feeling the pressure of attending Catholic Center almost immediately. I wanted to do really well in school because it wasn't every day. That a public school kid got to go to a fancy private school as CC. And I'm also thinking of all of the money that my father has and will spend. The schoolwork was a lot harder than what I was used too. I was used to getting A's and B's without even trying but now I'm studying really hard and I would be lucky to get a good grade.

Then I started noticing between classes that I wasn't seeing any girls. One time while at my locker I asked a guy 'where are the girls?' 'You don't know?' 'Know what?' 'This is an all-boys school.' 'What the hell, but I seen girls on my visit.' 'Those were probably cheerleaders that we use for our sport teams.'

After a few weeks of basketball practice with the JV Basketball team. I was promoted to the Varsity Basketball team. And during my first practice with the Varsity team. I'm running a play that the coach called Carolina. And the play called for me, the shooting guard to pass the ball into the block to the power forward.

Chapter 27 All 12 1/2

I was dribbling the basketball at the top of the key. When I threw a no-look pass to the forward. The basketball hit him in the chest, and he begin having an asthma attack. The coach saw that and blew his whistle. And got mad at me saying 'stop hot dogging, and get to the bench,' as I walked to the bench. While on the bench I'm confused because I didn't do anything wrong. So, the next day at practice I'm running all of the plays. And one play called for me to either drive to the rim or shoot a mid-range jumper. Now our bench players were defending and as I'm dribbling. I crossed over the player that was defending me and drove to the rim and scored. The coach blew his whistle and called for me, so when I got near I'm told 'stop playing like a colored kid.' And I asked, 'stop playing like a what?' 'You heard me McGee.' Now that happened near the end of practice, so I just walked off of the court. And while I was walking towards the locker room. I could hear coach calling me to come back, but I didn't. Then after changing my clothes and catching the bus home. Once home I told my mother about what happened at school and she said, 'maybe he doesn't know that your black.' 'That shouldn't even matter mom.' 'I bet that's what it is, Sergio he doesn't know.'

Then at the next practice I threw another no-look pass and before he could blow his whistle. I just went to the bench on my own. While sitting on the bench I'm trying to figure out what's going on with coach. Once on the bus to go home I'm still thinking about the situation with coach.Then I thought to myself that coach must be prejudiced. Now I remember being told stories about how it was when my mother grew up, but I had never experienced anything like that myself at that time. I continued to play basketball, but I no longer started. I only got to start whenever we played against African American schools.

Out of my frustration and thinking it would be different on the football team. I ended up trying out for the football team, and I made the team as a first string Middle Linebacker. Now I'm on both teams so that meant I had to attend both practices. And I found that really hard especially whenever I had to attend both practices on the same day. I would get to school around 7:15 am but I wouldn't leave until 7 pm or sometimes later. And on those nights I would have to walk home because the bus was no longer running. And that walk home would take me almost two hours.

The longer I went to Catholic Center. The more I would experience racism. I remember walking to class and I would have students come up to me asking me to speak. And when I said 'why' they would start laughing and started commenting that I had an accent because I sounded 'black'.

Whenever I would go to the cafeteria for lunch. It would look like a Civil Rights photo from the 60s. All 12 1/2 Africa American students athletes sat at that same table out of more than 2,400 students. And I was the 1/2 African American athlete. I felt that all of the African American athletes were only there to help the school win games.

Chapter 28 'In About 5 Minutes'

While sitting at that lunch table I became pretty close with most of the African American athletes, so much so. That it started showing on the football field and basketball court. We had gained a better understanding if you will on what was going on, so we started playing even harder but not for the school but for one another.

Mr. Randell my health teacher was also the wrestling coach. And one day after class he asked if I could do him a favor. So, I asked, 'what is it?' 'I need someone to wrestle at 165 pounds. And I've been having to forfeit all season. Then he asked what did I weigh?' 'About 162 pounds why?' 'That's great so will you do it?' 'Do what?' 'Wrestle' 'I can't. I'm already playing two sports, so I'm sorry.' 'Come on, Sergio there are only 11 matches left you could do this!' 'I don't know any wrestling moves, so I'm sorry.' 'I'll teach you some moves.' 'I can't I'm sorry,' as he kept pleading and I finally agreed to wrestle 'that's great.' Then I asked, 'so when will I learn some moves?' "Just come in tomorrow after basketball practice.' Then I asked 'so when is my first match?' 'In 2 days,' 'but I don't know any moves.' Then after basketball practice, I learned only two moves and I wasn't able to learn any more because of my other two sports games and practice.

The day of the match I walked into the gym with some shorts and a t-shirt on. Then the coach handed me a 1 piece and said, 'put this on now.' 'Why?' 'This is what everyone wears,' so I reluctantly walked back into the locker room. Once dressed, I walked back into the gym as I'm looking around for the ring, but I didn't see one, so I asked the coach 'where's the ring?' 'What ring?' 'Oh, you're thinking about television that's not real wrestling. You have to wrestle on this,' as he pointed to the blue mat on the floor. 'Who am I fighting or wrestling,' as he pointed across the gym while saying 'that school.' 'When do I wrestle?' 'In about 5 minutes, so are you ready to wrestle?' 'I guest with only knowing two moves.'

Now it's time for me to wrestle, as I nervously walked out onto the floor and mat. The referee went over the rules and he checked my fingernails. Then he told me to get down on all four and I asked, 'why?' So, Coach Randell came out to the mat as I'm standing there, and I'm told 'you have to get down on your hands and knees that's how we start.' The referee gave some more instructions and I reluctantly got down on my hands and knees, as the referee moved out of the way and said, 'go.' The guy that I was wrestling jumped onto my back and he's trying to pin me. I was able to reverse a lot of his moves, so that allowed me to win the match. And coach was more than excited while saying 'I knew that you had it in you, Sergio!' I had won ten of my matches, but I had one more match to go. With this polar bear sized kid from Garden City High School. I looked towards my coach, as he just smiled and said, 'you can do this!' I walked out to the mat and I looked up at this giant man child. The referee went over the instructions as I'm looking for some kind of weakness. The referee moved and said, 'go,' as the man child got on top of me and he put me into some kind of arm lock, that I manage to get out of. Now I'm on top of him, as I struggled to get him pinned. It's the final round and I assumed that I was losing. After several back and forth the referee jumped in and screamed 'it's over,' as I stood up and we shook hands. The referee announced him to be the winner and I walked away with my head held low, as coach approached.

Chapter 29 Our Telephone

'There's no reason for you to lower your head, Sergio. You've won ten out of eleven matches and you don't even wrestle.' With the amount of pressure that I was feeling while attending Catholic Center. I started thinking that this isn't worth it. I'm dealing with things that I shouldn't have to and I'm feeling that I no longer wish to go to CC but it's January, so I'm trying to make it through the school year. And with all of the racisms that I was experiencing and all the money that's being spent. And my own pressure of wanting to do well, so I talked with my sister about how I was feeling. And she told me 'you need to do what's best for you and not everyone else, Sergio,' and I agreed.

So, once all of my sports were completed, and with only weeks left in the school year. I walked into my counselor's office. And I told him that I no longer wish to attend Catholic Center. He seemed surprised and asked, 'why?' I didn't say everything, but I did mention the racism and he asked, 'is there anything that I could do to help you with this?' 'I don't think so sir I'm sorry I don't think there's anything that you or anyone could do.' After I told him what I had to say we shook hands and I walked out of his office. I knew that would be my last time in that school.

And once I got home, I told my mother about what I had done. 'Are you sure, Sergio?' 'I'm positive I've already spoke with my counselor.' 'You need to call and tell your father. 'I know I will.' Then I called my auntie Dana and I told her that I would no longer need a ride. Then I had to find another high school to attend and according to my address. I should be able to attend the neighborhood RedFord High School.

Once the time came, I walked several blocks up to the school to enroll. After waiting three hours in line I'm told that I needed another paper that I didn't have so I leave. The next day I walked back up there with the paper that I needed. And after two hours of waiting in line I'm told that I need another paper, so I went home to get the paper, and walked back up to the school in the rain. I got into the line with all of the papers that I needed. Once at the front of the line I gave all of my papers to the lady behind the table. She looked over my papers and told me to go to the next table. Once at the front of that line, as I handed my papers to the lady that was supper mean. And she asked, 'did you just move or are you a trans?' 'What's a trans?' 'When you're changing schools.' 'Okay, then I'm transferring' and she asked for my papers. And after looking at them she handed me a paper and I'm told to go to the next table. Once in the front of that line I gave the lady my papers. And after a few minutes I'm giving my schedule with classroom numbers and teachers names.

Once home I told my mother that I'm finally in there now. 'That's good, Sergio but you still haven't told your father.' 'I haven't yet,' so I walked several blocks to use the payphone because our telephone had been turned off. While I'm walking, I'm trying to figure out what to tell him, so I decided to just tell him the truth. When he answered the telephone. "I'm calling from a payphone,' as he interrupted and asking, 'are you okay?' 'I'm fine our telephone got turned off.' I told him that I have some bad news and he asked, 'what is it?'

Chapter 30 It's The 2nd Semester

'I've decided not to go back to Catholic Center,' 'so what's the bad news?' 'That was the bad news.' 'Okay, so where will you go now?' 'I've enrolled myself into RedFord High School.' I was really surprised by his responses until he said, 'I'll save some money now.' And that's when I knew the reason why he didn't mind but I was just glad that he wasn't disappointed in me. But as I look back at that now I'm disappointed in myself because I wish I would've handled that situation a lot better. On my walk back home. I felt a lot better because I had finally told him and I wasn't feeling that burden of weight on my shoulders anymore.

Now it was the day before school at RedFord and I had set out my clothes for tomorrow morning. I was really excited to be wearing normal clothes again. I woke up around 6:20 am and I took my shower and got dressed in my iron crease blue Levis jeans, and a matching jacket. With my blue and red Adidas t-shirt and red white and blue top ten Adidas gym shoes. Once ready I walked a few houses down my street to my friend Stan's house. He was in the 11th grade and I was in the 10th. While socializing with him and his friends. A lot of people at school assumed I was in their grade. The first couple of months of school was great. I'm getting good grades because the schoolwork was a lot easier. While in the hallways I'm trying not to be noticed as I'm looking at every girl.

After a while I found myself in the same situation that I was dealing with while at Emerson Middle School. I saw some of the same guys that would come to fight me at Emerson in the hallway. I had forgotten that they went to RedFord until I saw some of them in the hallway. And most of them are seniors now and a couple of the guys lived a few blocks behind me. And I knew that one of the guys was hustling, so I just assumed that he was packing heat.

It's the 2nd semester and I had to change my classes. And one of the guys that I was beefing with from Emerson is now in my second hour class. And on the very first day that we were in class together.

Chapter 31 I Wasn't Believing Him

He started talking shit in front of everyone. But that really didn't bother me because we had fought before and I was getting the best of him until the others jumped in. The one thing that I've learned over the years. The person with the most mouth is usually the weakest one. But surprisingly I made it through the first year without having to fight.

Now it was summertime and I was looking for a real job. My uncle Lamar was a supervisor for a janitorial service. So, I called and asked him if he had any kind of work for me? 'Let me take a look and see if I have something available." After a few weeks he called and said that he has something. Then told me 'you're 19 and not 15 years old okay?' The job was at the historic Northland Mall. He told me that we'll be stripping and waxing the mall before the holidays. 'I'll be picking you up tomorrow at 8:30 pm okay?' 'Okay I'll be ready.'

The next evening, he arrived, and we drove to the mall. Once at the mall we waited near the delivery door for the other guys to arrive. Once they arrived, we entered the mall. My uncle told me and his oldest son my cousin Ron. That he wanted us to scrape all of the floors before the other guys stripped and waxed them. One day while working I walked over to where Ron was working. When I got near the area, I saw him dragging clothes through a store gate. I walked up and said, 'what the hell are you doing you're going to get us fired'! 'Were not going to get fired, Sergio. I've been doing this for a couple of days, but don't tell my father.' 'If he finds out about this, he's going to kill you. I don't want any part of this,' as I walked away. The next day I saw my cousin doing it again but this time I seen how. He was using the scraper and he would put it through the gate. Then he would knock the clothes off the rack and drag the clothes through the gate. Once I saw that I went and found and told his father our boss.'The only reason I'm telling you this is because I don't want the rest of us to get fired.' After telling him he said he was glad that I told him, then he asked, 'where is he now?' After telling him where Ron was. We started walking over to his side of the mall.

Once there Ron was scraping the floor. When my uncle asked, 'what's this I hear about you stealing?' While looking surprised and said, 'what are you talking about I haven't stolen anything'! 'So, Sergio is lying?' After they argued for a while he told Ron 'you're fired,' as Ron looked at me while shaking his head and walked away. 'I'm really glad that you told because they have cameras with microphones all throughout this mall. We all would've been fired, and your cousin would be in jail, so thank you but get back to work.'

Weeks later he asked me to help him move a bench, so I grabbed the other end of the bench. And he told me to push the bench towards him, so I pushed and I had to push the bench a little harder to get it over some floor tiles. Once clearing the tiles, the bench picked up speed. And the bench pushed into my uncle and he ended up going back first into a shoe store display window. With several long pieces of glass dangling over him. And when he set up inside of the display window, as I looked and took off running. While running I could hear him calling my name but I just kept running. While trying to get as far away as possible. After running to the other side of the mall. I could still hear him calling my name and he seemed to be getting closer. He made his way near where I was and said, 'I'm not going to jump on you, Sergio,' but I wasn't believing him. 'I'm okay, Sergio it's not your fault. I'm not going to keep chasing you. Now get your ass back to work' and he walked away.

Chapter 32 I See You Already Know

I waited a good ten minutes before walking back to my work area. Then on the ride home that morning I was super quiet, as he did all the talking. 'I didn't think you were going to get into the car, Sergio,' as he started laughing. That job lasted about eight weeks. And with the money that I made from that job and hustling. I was able to put some clothes into a lay away.

It's about three weeks before school when Stan told me about our friend from school that's working at a clothing store. 'He can hook us up with some clothes. We just need to go up there while he's at work and he'll do the rest.' I drove up there with Stan and once in the store we started shopping. I'm told get whatever you would buy and just get into his line' so I filled my cart. Once I got into the line at his register. I began counting up the items in my cart. Once at the register I acted like I didn't know him. After ringing up my clothes I paid about 200 dollars. Although I had well over 400 dollars' worth of clothes. With the money that I saved I was able to get my brothers some clothes and shoes also.

One day while walking to the liquor store on GrandRiver and Lasher. I noticed an ABC drivers' school across the street, so after leaving the store. I walked across the street where I saw a sign in the window. That read 99 dollars & 2 weeks, so I walked in and spoke with the instructor. And I signed up and paid for the class.

Once I started driving school, I purchased myself an old hoop-tie for 500 dollars. I would drive the school's car every other day, as part of the class. While driving the instructor would always remind me to do 10 and 2 on the steering wheel. 'I see you already know how to drive,' as I'm driving. 'But do you know the information needed to pass the Secretary of State test?' 'I'm not sure' 'and that's were I come in I will teach you everything that you'll need to know so you'll pass that test.'

Chapter 33 'That's Some Bullshit'

Once I graduated from ABC drivers' school. I went to get my driver's license at the Secretary of State. I didn't have to take the road test because of my on the road driving. After passing I was given a green piece of paper that allowed me to be able to drive. Until my driver's license arrived in the mail.

It was back to school time and I would get up take my shower and get dressed. Then I would walk over to Stan's house, as we walked to school like last year. Once inside of the school as all of the students had to line up. The school was having a weapons sweep. After being searched I went to my locker. Where I saw one of the guys that I had been beefing with. And he started talking shit so I just walked away. Once in class I had girls telling me 'there's some guys talking about fighting you. I just thought that you should know.' 'Thank you, but I'm not worried about that.' Then I'm told 'you should be, Sergio there's a lot of them.' Now I'm thinking how she knew, or did they put her up to this.

After class I went to one of my lockers on the second floor to get a book, as a guy pushed me from behind. I turned around, as the guy started yelling, 'how come you're white and all these black girls like you,' so I punched him. And as he was stumbling and fell up against the lockers across the hall. As I walked towards him and was looking down at him and said, 'how come you're black and they don't like your ass' and walked away. I'm thinking that couldn't be what the girl was talking about so now I'm still looking for something else to happen.

Once school let out and I'm outside waiting on Stan. When he came out and we started walking home. I decided to tell him about my situation in school. 'I already knew but thanks for telling me.' 'How did you know?' 'I've been going here a lot longer than you and I hear things,' as we started laughing.

Now I've switched classes, so I'm on my way to my fifth hour class. That's Spanish were an attractive girl named Monique that I always seemed to sit next to. She looked to be biracial and we would flirt a lot, so much so. That even the teacher once said, 'you two would make a cute couple.' After a while I asked, 'would you mind dating me?' 'No but I think there's something that you should know first.' 'What's that?' 'I have a daughter and her father goes to this school.' 'I don't have a problem with that do you?' 'I don't I just thought that you should know.' After a while she showed me the guy and I laughed. While saying 'him?' 'Yeah, I know,' as she laughed. 'He just doesn't look like the kind of guy that you would fuck with let alone have a baby with, but wow'!

Then shortly after while at my locker. The guy walked up to me and tapped me on my shoulder. When I turned around, I didn't recognize him at first. 'So, you're the great Sergio.' 'Yes, I am why?' 'So, you're the one I've been earring about that's so great.' 'Well depending on who you ask I am great.' Then when I recognized him and said, 'I'm defiantly better than you. I've done more for your daughter then you have.' 'I'm in school so I can't do anything for her right now.' 'That's some bullshit shit she didn't ask to be here,' as he started stuttering. So, I pushed him up against the locker and told him. 'You need to do everything that you can for that little girl' and I walked away.

Chapter 34 'Is She Coming Back'

The next day in Spanish class Monique told me that he came over yesterday to see her daughter. And he even brought her diapers and he's never done that before.' ' That's nice,' 'so what did you do, Sergio?' 'What do you mean?' 'I pointed him out to you and all of a sudden he comes over, so what did you do?' While laughing 'I don't know what you're talking about.' 'Whatever, Sergio I know you, you did something.'

Then later that year my mother started dating this man that I didn't care for, so he came over on a Friday night. Once I heard him, I came downstairs to get something to drink. And I also wanted him to know that she wasn't home alone. When I came out of the kitchen, I saw that he had his foot on the table, so I asked, 'could you remove your foot from the table,' as I stood there. He looked up at me then looked away but left his foot on the table. I said again 'can you take your foot off of my table and I'm not asking again.' 'Oh, so it's your table now?' "Yeah it is, I bought everything in here.' He looked away but never removed his foot, so I stepped in front of him and punched him in his head. Then we started fighting and that fight went from the living room to outside. And in front of the house was a big tree and during the fight I rammed his head into the tree. He fell onto the ground and my mother came outside while screaming 'leave him alone,' as he got up and stumbled to his car. I yelled 'why are you crying over him, you want to be with him that bad?' 'Yes, I do' and I couldn't believe that she said that, so I went into the house. And I gathered most of her clothes and put them into several garbage bags. Then I went to the screen door and tossed the bags onto the sidewalk and said, 'then you can go be with him,' as she grabbed the bags, and they drove off. As I'm left standing on the porch in disbelief. I couldn't believe that she choose a man over her children.

Once in the house my brothers came up to me asking 'where did mommy go?' 'Is she coming back?' 'She'll be back don't worry everything will be fine,' as I put them back to bed. Then I went into my bedroom and slammed the door.

Once I got into my bed, I'm thinking on why she would do this, as I cried myself to sleep. The next morning, I went downstairs and I'm thinking of what all I have to do now. My mother is gone, and we all have school on Monday.

Chapter 35 I Decided

I gathered all of the bills, as I'm trying to figure out what all has to be paid. I knew the rent was 350 dollars a month, because I used to get money orders for my mom. The light and gas bills combined was about 140 dollars a month. The water bill was 30 dollars every three months. The telephone bill was about 90 dollars a month. So, now that I knew how much money I will need every month. But I also have to factor in food and other expenses for me and my brothers. Then I got a telephone call from Monique my girlfriend at that time. And she's telling me about being frustrated and how she was leaving her parents' home. I interrupted and told her 'just come over here and stay with me.' Then she asked, 'but what will your mother say?' And I told her about what happened last night, and she said, 'okay I'll call you when I get a ride.' I told her 'just take a cab and I'll pay when you get here.' 'Okay.' And Monique arrived within an hour and I went outside to pay.

Once inside after putting her infant daughter into my bed. We went back downstairs and started talking. Then she asked, 'do you think that you can do this, Sergio?' 'I don't have a choice but to be able to do this.' 'I'm so proud of you for doing this.' 'I just know that I need to get another job and hustle even more.' So after Monique agreed to stay. We started talking about how this could be done. Our plan became Monique would stay home with my brothers. And she would cook and clean while I worked two jobs, went to school and hustled. Things took a while to become routine but once it did everything seemed to operate smooth. From time to time my brothers would ask 'when is mommy coming back home?' And after a while I sat them down and just told them. 'I don't know when she's coming back' and they began crying. 'But I do know that she will be back.' And that was hard to tell them. And again I'm fifteen doing all of this while attending high school working two jobs, and hustling.

And with everything that was going on at that time I decided that I would drop out of school. My thought was I would have more time to make more money. So, in October I decided to drop out of school but I didn't tell anyone I just stopped going to class. I didn't want to drop out of school but I just felt it was the best thing for me to do at that time. I found a place in the shadows of the old Tigers Stadium.

Chapter 36 The Window

Where I could take a GED test and I believe I paid 50 dollars. I completed the test in two days and I received a very high score in the 90% range. Now I was happy about having my GED but it's not a diploma.

Now both of my jobs were at restaurants. On my first job I had worked my way up from busting tables to becoming a Sauté Cook. Then I bought myself a beeper so Monique and certain money could reach me. I also worked across the parking lot at another restaurant. And both restaurants jobs were located in Southfield, Michigan. Where a lot of young caucasian college students worked. And a lot of those students became some of my best customers. I would charge them extra money for their drugs and they didn't mind paying because they wanted their drugs from Detroit. I worked there for several years but all good things must come to an end. So, I ended up quitting both jobs. And I would just work with my uncle Lamar some and hustle.One day while in my bedroom I heard the front door open. So, I got up and walked downstairs to see what made that noise.

Once down most of the steps I saw a shadow of someone walking into the dining room. Once I got into the living room where I could see that it was my mother and she's sitting at the dining room table. So I asked, 'what are you doing here?' And she just said 'I'm back.' 'So, you just think that you can just leave for almost a year and just walk back in here like you never left?' But she wouldn't say anything, and I assumed that my brothers heard her voice or me yelling at her, as they came running down the stairs and onto our mother arms, as they started hugging and kissing on her. While I just stood there feeling frustrated. I knew they were excited to see our mother, but I had questions and I wasn't getting any answers. But knowing my mother there's a reason for her return.

So, I went back into my bedroom and I slammed the door. And Monique asked, 'what's that about?' 'My mother is back,' as I sat on the bed near Monique. Then she asked, 'did she ever say why,' as I interrupted. And said, 'I tried to ask but all she would say is I'm back. Then my brothers came down and started hugging and kissing on her.' 'What do you expect, Sergio, that's their mother.' 'I understand that, but she ran out on us over a man.' 'Did you hear yourself?' 'Yeah I said she ran out on them.' 'No, Sergio you said on us.' 'Whatever you know what I meant.' 'I guess I'll get my stuff together now to leave.' 'For what?' 'Because I don't want any trouble.' 'You're not going anywhere you're staying right here with me.' 'Are you sure because I can always go back to my parents?' 'It's not like you don't know my mother. Hell, she likes you more compared to my other girls,' as Monique hit me on my arm. 'Ouched! Why did you hit me?' 'Your other girls, really Sergio.' I knew what she was thinking about when she said that because a few months earlier. A girl that I had been messing around with stood outside of my opened bedroom window. And started yelling things like 'he's messing with me too girl.' And once Monique heard that she tried to get outside to fight. Then the girl yelled 'he was over my house the other night hitting this really good'.

Chapter 37 Until It Ended

After about 30 minutes of yelling things the girl leaves. Then I'm asked, 'who the fuck was that bitch?' I lied 'I don't know.' 'How did she know your house and bedroom window?' I lied again 'I don't know I'm out here hustling every day, so maybe someone told her.' After arguing and answering all of Monique questions. We finally went back to bed but I wasn't going asleep. Until I knew that she was asleep first.

And after a few months. Monique went back to stay with her parents. Although she said, 'this isn't about that girl.' But I knew that played a big part. We still remained a couple and would hang out and sleep together, but things just weren't the same until it ended.

Then shortly after one day I was walking home from my sister's house. When I saw some of my friends standing in the middle of the street. They stopped me and told me how they had formed a rap group named 1st Class, but I wasn't in the group. I was wondering why they didn't include me but I didn't say anything. And once home I decided to form a rap group of my own.

Chapter 38 Golden Records

I've always received awards in school for writing short stories and poems. But trying to write a rhyme is something different. I dugout some of my rap albums like RUN DMC & LL COOL J. I put them on my record player and I listened to them for hours. Then I decided to write down some lyrics, but my lyrics didn't have any kind of structure. So, I went back and listened to my albums again. And I learned that most rap songs had 16 bars per verse and a bar is a written lyric, that rhymes with the following lyric. I also notice that most rap songs would have 3 or 4 verses and each verse had 16 bars.

Once I discovered the structure, I started writing songs. I didn't have a name for my group, so I started writing down different names. I choose Raw Deal for my group name, but I didn't have a name for myself. After writing down several names. I picked IROC but not because I liked the car, but because I rock at this. I didn't want to spell it the same as the car or how it sounded so I dropped the K.

After a few days of practicing I went outside, and I saw my friends 1st Class. When I walked over to where they were. One of the guys was rhyming, so I listened. And his lyrics were good but I thought mine were better. After he recited a few of his verses I decided to give it a try and I started spitting what I had wrote. And once done they couldn't believe that I could flow. They keep telling me how I need to record a demo.

So, we recorded our first demo at the same studio on the same day. I took a 12 inch instrumental of a record that I had been rehearsing to. And other then some drums and different sounds. I pretty much just rhymed over that instrumental. That demo became my first song that I titled 'Turn it Up.' I got a guy that lived around the corner to become my deejay. Now I had my own rap group. And after a year or so 1st Class asked me to join their group. After joining it's 3 rappers and 1 deejay. And one of the rappers was asking me to write all of his verses. Then he decided that he wanted to become a deejay so we made the change. Now it's 2 rappers and 2 deejays and we performed at every show possible. And that lasted for several years but I just felt that we weren't doing enough as a group, so I decided to become a solo artist again. That was a very hard decision to make. We were already good friends and between rehearsing, doing shows and recording. I just felt even closer to them.

Although that change was hard but I felt that it was also necessary. And my friend Stan also left 1st Class and became my deejay. And after a performance a man dressed in an airbrushed denim trench coat came up and introduced himself as Mr. Gold. He told me that he liked my song but the music could've been better. 'I produce tracks that you should be rapping too. I also have my own recording studio so come through and check me out,' as he gave me his business card. After about two weeks I called and was told to come through so he gave me the address.

Once I arrived at the address. I saw that it was a house, so I pulled into the driveway. And once out of my car I knocked on the front door and Mr. Gold answered the door and invited me into the house. Once in the house he said, 'follow me,' as we walked into the basement. Once I got into the basement, I saw that he had constructed a recording studio and sound both on one side of the basement. Then he sat in front of a counter of equipment and started playing tracks that he produced. And with the reasonable rate that he was charging to record. I started coming through to record my demos.

One day while recording he asked 'what's your plans with this music?' "I would like to get a record deal but why do you ask?' 'What if I could do that for you what would you say?' 'Let's do it.' 'I have my own record label "Golden Records." I want to put together a compilation album with all of my artist. Then shop that compilation album to get a major record deal. What do you think about that?' 'If I was to sign, I must keep creative control over my music. Also, over whatever else I was to do.' 'That's fine with me,' as he went behind the curtain in the basement and got a 1-page contract. And that's how I became a recording artist on Golden Records.

And he would have meetings at his house once a month. With all of the artists that he signed or wanted to sign. There would be at least 25 people there or more and everyone there either rapped, danced , sing or deejayed. There was some of the best talent in Detroit at those meetings. It became like a large family atmosphere. I'm still friends with some of the same people that I meant there over 25 years ago. I believe with the talent on Golden Records. It could had been just as big or bigger than No Limit or Bad Boy Records. And Golden Records released a compilation album that was titled "Knowledge is Power." I had a song on the album titled "I'm Everlasting." I did everything that I was contracted and asked to do while on that label. Then after a performance at what I believe was the Latin Quarters. I asked my friend/bodyguard "Big Deal" to drop me off. Over to a friend and record label mat house that I was living with at that time that we called Surgeon.

Chapter 39 'I'm Going To Try To Save You'

This was a night that I will never forget. I was in the living room sitting on the couch. Writing because I had a show on that Saturday. It's Wednesday morning around 2 am on April 17th 1990. When suddenly I heard the window behind me just shatter and I started getting riddled with bullets. I looked up and saw the arcade game that was in the corner of the living room just explode. As the mirrors on the dining room wall just started shattering, as they fell onto the floor. Now during that hectic time, I decided to get up and try to make it into the back bedroom. Once I stood up and I was ducking trying not to get shot in the head. I took a few small steps around a coffee table. When I was struck with a thundering shot that literally knocked me to my knees. I manage to keep moving, as I crawled into the dining room. While crawling through the dining room. I'm shot at again through the kitchen window that faced the dining room. There was a table placed in front of that window and on that table was an old metal toaster. And when I heard the shot, I looked up at the window. And I saw a huge hole in that toaster. I truly believe I would've got shot again if not for that toaster. It felt like I was in a war movie with bullets just flying around and everything just shattering or exploding.

I finally made it into the back bedroom and I collapsed onto the floor. While in tremendous pain and my heart was pounding out of my chest. Without realizing I started taking deep breaths to help slow down my blood flow. That's something that I learned while playing multiple sports in high school. While on the bedroom floor I saw the telephone, so I began to reach for the telephone. Once I grabbed the cord, I dragged the telephone towards me. And instead of calling 911 like I should've I tried to call my auntie, and I dialed the wrong number. I was really hesitating about calling her at first because I knew that she heard about me hustling. Once she answered the telephone, I told her that I had been shot. And she asked, 'what hospital are you in?' 'I'm not in a hospital, I'm still on the floor of the house where I got shot.' I'm not sure how that conversation ended, but I hung up the telephone. With smoke coming from everywhere that I had been shot and I'm smelling the foul order of my burning flesh.

After a while one of the guys that was at the house appeared in the doorway. And said, 'oh shit Roc been hit' and he grabbed the telephone and called 911. While I'm lying on the floor as I waited on an ambulance to arrive. And I'm thinking about what just happened and I'm feeling that this maybe my demise as my pain level seemed to decrease. Then I quickly changed my thoughts and my pain level seemed to increase.

Then after what seemed to be 30 minutes or more. I saw an EMT come into the bedroom but he's alone. Then he looked down at me with a "you're fucked" look on his face and said, 'I'll be right back I'm going to go get my partner' and leaves. I'm thinking why isn't your partner with you. Then they returned with a yellow stretcher and as they're getting me onto the stretcher. I then heard a police officer that was standing near the bedroom door. And he asked, 'what happened to you?' I looked up at him in disbelief and said, 'what the hell does it look like I've been shot you can see that right?' Then he said, 'I need to ask you a few questions.' And I said, 'wow really' as I shook my head and said, 'I'm trying to live right now, so your damn questions can wait,' as I'm carried out of the bedroom.

Once they got me near the front door. I could hear them whispering 'there's blood dripping through the stretcher' and I'm taken and placed inside of the back of the ambulance. As I'm lying there, I closed my eyes and begin praying. When the EMT that was in the back with me started yelling saying 'what's your name?' as I opened my eyes and said, 'my name is Sergio and y'all taking too damn long to get me to the hospital.' Then I'm told 'I'm going to try to save you' and I looked up and said, 'wow really you're going to try thanks, as I closed my eyes and started praying again. In my prayer I'm asking God to let me survive. I have a child on the way and I want to be there to see my child. And I don't want another man helping in raising my child. I also promised God that I wouldn't seek any vengeance on those that shot me I just want to live. The house where I got shot was located on Washburn Street near Puritan Avenue.

Chapter 40 You Still Have A Lot Of Blood

The ambulance took the pothole riddled Lodge freeway to the hospital. And with every bump my pain level increased even more. I finally arrived at Sini Grace Hospital and that's the year the two hospitals had merged. I was rushed into an ER room where I'm placed onto a hospital table. While lying there, I could hear a doctor asking for blood stat. Then I heard another female doctor say, 'we're not going to use any of the hospital blood.' I'm thinking take the damn blood. Then she said, 'were going to use his blood plasma to make blood. That way we don't have to worry about HIV infection.' Then a doctor started cutting off my clothes and he removed my jewelry. Then he started digging his fingers into my bullet wounds as I screamed terribly. Then another doctor placed a Nasal Mask over my face and told me to breath. So, I started breathing because I'm thinking it was oxygen. Then I heard a doctor say, 'he should be out, but he isn't' and that's when I realized that it wasn't oxygen but anesthesia. Then I heard the doctors talking saying 'I've giving him 17 hits and with a man of his size. It should've only taken 3 or 4 hits.' Then I started feeling some nominees in my legs and it traveled into my stomach. I thought I was dying, so I somewhat set up and kicked two nurses that were near my feet. And punched a doctor, and my IVs came out of my arms. Then I saw the green curtain that surrounded the hospital table that I was on fall, and I just passed out.

I was told that my surgery lasted more than five hours. And I was only giving a 40 % chance to survive the surgery. After surviving surgery I was placed into their ICU. After taking so much anesthesia they weren't able to awake me after surgery. So, It took me almost two days for me to awake on my own. The doctor that performed my surgery came into my room and told me 'you've been shot six times. With an AK47 a 12 gauge and a 9 millimeter from about ten feet away or less. And your left lung has collapsed.' I tried to respond but I couldn't speak. The doctor realized that I couldn't speak and said, 'that sometimes happened after surgery with anesthesia.'

The next morning two doctors came into my ICU room. And said, 'we have to put this tube into your lung. And we're going to do this now and I can't put you under anesthesia because I need for you to hold your breath as I'm inserting the tube, so can you do that?' I just shook my head saying yes. The doctor rubbed some iodine on my left side and pulled out a scalable and said. 'Once I get to the number 3, I'll need for you to hold your breath until I'm done.' Then he started counting '1 2 3,' as he started cutting and I could feel him running that tube across my ribs and into my lung. Not to mention the pain that I was feeling while I'm being cut open. That tube was connected to a pump that stood near my bed. Once done I was told that I could breath as I took a large gasp of breath.

Then later that day a male X-ray tech came into my room. He wanted to get some X-rays of my left shoulder. I heard the nurse tell him about what was just done, and she said, 'so please be careful.' I heard him tell the nurse that 'I'll be careful.' Then he walked over towards my bed and set up his equipment. He never introduced himself which I thought was weird, because everyone else had. Then he pulled out a white board to place behind my shoulder. Then he aggressively yanked me up by my shoulder and valiantly shoved the board behind my shoulder. I'm in tremendous pain and pissed, as I waited for him to finish. Once he took that board from behind my shoulder. I took my right hand and swung as hard as I could. And I punched him in his noise. And my IVs came out and that alerted the nurse. When the nurse came in, she saw the guy noise was bleeding, so she asked, 'what happen?' I heard him say 'that guy just punched me,' as he pointed at me. She looked at my bandage and saw blood coming through. 'I thought I asked you to be careful.' 'I was.' 'You couldn't have I see blood on his bandage, so I know you weren't.' I was so glad that she could tell what happened. After redoing my bandage I'm told 'I don't blame you for hitting him hell I would've also.'

Then later that day I'm able to have visitors and my mother walked in and I began crying. And she wiped my tears and told me 'you'll be alright stop crying.' I just wanted to apologize to her for this happening and to tell her that I love her. Then she told me 'I know I know, so stop crying' and for the first time since being a small child. It felt like an authentic mother and son moment. She talked with me for about 20 minutes. Then told me 'I called your father and he's up here drunk and acting a fool so I'm going to leave so your father can come in' and she walked out of the room.

My father came in and said, 'I can't stay long I just wanted to come see you.' And I'm thinking you can't stay long and I'm your only child. Then he said, 'you'll be fine you're a strong kid and I'll see you soon champ,' as he walked out of the room. I'm thinking why would he drive an hour or more just to visit me for three minutes. I knew that he was drunk because I could smell the liquor on him.

Then after he leaves my sister walked in and my tears started rolling down my face. She sat in the chair that's next to my bed. And said, 'don't be trying to die on me,' as she hit me on my leg. So now I'm really crying as I'm trying to speak. Then she grabbed my hand and for whatever reason I started writing words inside of her palm. And she understood everything that I wrote. I was so excited to be communicating again that I kept writing I'm sorry. And she said, 'stop saying you're sorry, Sergio you didn't shoot yourself.' And she was at that hospital with me like she was a patient. It wasn't until I asked her to please go home and maybe take a shower. Because I know you will feel a lot better. And she said, 'I'll go home when you go home, Sergio.' So, after three days at 24-hours a day she finally went home.

The next day I was surprised to see Renee. The young lady that was about 7 months pregnant with our child. She walked into my room and sat in the chair next to my bed. As I struggled to hold back my tears. Once she realized that I couldn't speak she started talking and I keep staring at her stomach. When she stood up and was about to leave, I placed my right hand onto her stomach, and I said a quick prayer. Once she left out of the room I started uncontrollably crying as I thought about my unborn child.

After a day or so I was moved out of ICU and into a regular hospital room. And shortly after being in that room an older African American female nursing assistant. Came into the room to see if I needed anything and said, 'I'll be right back,' as she leaves. Then she returned with soap and towels and said, 'it looks like they didn't clean you up after your surgery. You still have a lot of blood all over you, but don't worry I'll clean you up.' I'm able to speak now as I thanked here. After bathing me and changing my gown I thanked here again and she left.

Chapter 41 'Just Give Us The Word Roc'

I assumed there was a shift change. Because the nursing assistant that I had now were a lot closer to my age. The young African Americans ladies came into my room to see if I needed anything. I said, 'no I'm fine, but thank you.' And the one young lady said, 'wow you're so polite,' as they left.

Then later that afternoon the same two nursing assistants came into my room. And they started gossiping and watching my television. While gossiping one assistant asked the other 'did you hear about the Detroit rapper that got shot and killed the other day?' Once I heard that I started paying attention. I'm thinking maybe I know the rapper. Then she said, 'someone named Rock' and I didn't say anything but there saying I'm dead.

The next day the doctor that performed my surgery came into my room. And said, 'you're a very lucky young man in my over 30 plus years of being a doctor. I've never seen someone that healed so quickly as you. I told you my name for you now is Wolverine,' as we laughed.

The next day I had a very unattractive obese caucasian nurse that came into my room. She looked at me and said, 'I'm going to wash you up.' I lied and said, 'I've already been washed up this morning.' 'Well I'm going to wash you up again,' as she leaves to gather supplies. I knew that's something that nurses normally don't do. And when she returned, I kept saying 'I've already been washed up,' but she wasn't hearing it. I probably wouldn't have minded if she was an attractive woman. As I'm being washed, I just felt that I was being violated. She just seemed to enjoy bathing me too much.

The next morning, I saw and told my mother about what happened. And she said, 'I'll be right back,' as she went out of the room. I could hear her fussing and cursing at someone outside of my door. When she came back into my room and said, 'you don't have to worry about that bitch anymore.'

The next day several friends of mine came up to visit. 'We would've been up sooner but the hospital has you listed as a John Doe, so we didn't know where you were and we're going to kill whoever did this shit Roc and starting with your boy Surgeon. We know his ass had something to do with what happened, so just give us the word Roc and he's dead,' as I thought about my previous prayer and said, 'I don't want y'all killing or harming anyone,' as they physically seemed upset. 'I need y'all to promise me that,' as they reluctantly agreed to what I said. I remained in the hospital for a few more days. It would've been six days, but I had to wait for a doctor to return to work to sign for my release. After leaving the hospital I went over to my twin aunties' house that are nurses. I was there for two days as my aunties did my treatments.

Chapter 42 After A Few Days

When my other auntie Marie came over to visit. My aunties expressed how they didn't have the room for me to stay with them, but they didn't want me to go back to that house. My auntie Marie told them that I could come and stay with her and she'll take care of me. My twin aunties showed her how to do my treatments.

Then I went over to my auntie Marie's house. I was already familiar with being over her house. I would go over there a lot for cookouts or just to chill with her children and my cousins. My auntie has the smallest house out of my whole family. A 2 bedroom ranch style home on Pembroke Street near Lasher. But she volunteered for me to come over while knowing that she didn't have a lot of room either.

Once I got to her house, she told me 'you'll have to sleep in the basement.' 'That's fine I'm just glad that you're allowing me to stay.' 'You're fine honey.' My uncle Bill (my aunties husband) used the basement as a man cave. So, I would try to stay out of his way whenever he would watch games or fights. He also would get ready for work in the basement. And whenever he was down there, we would always talk about sports or just life in general.

I had gotten 75 staples down my stomach from where they removed some bullets from my diaphragm. My scar looks as if I had a C section. Also do to me being shot in my left biceps my arm was in a sling. I also had a huge bullet hole in my left shoulder area from where my AC joint was shattered. With multiple bandages all on my left side. My auntie would do my treatments every day. And she would always start with my shoulder. Then after slowly removing my old treatment. She would wipe saline around the large bullet hole. Then place an alcohol-soaked bandage inside of my bullet hole that would burn for several hours. Once done she would cover up my wound with a new bandage. And she would do something similar for my other wounds as well.

After a few days 'it's shower time.' And I said, 'I can't take a shower right now auntie.' 'I know that's why I'm going to help you, Sergio.' So, I went into the basement and put on some shorts. Then went back upstairs and got into the shower. She came into the bathroom and stood outside of the tub as she would help to wash me. That became our new routine until I was able to shower myself.

After a few months of being there on July 19th I got beep and when I called back. I was told that my son had been born so I got a ride up to the hospital. Once at Hutzel Hospital I inquired about her room and once told. I walked to and entered Renee's room, as I slowly opened the door. When I saw Renee holding our son in her arms, so I walked over to her bedside and asked, 'how are you doing?' 'I'm better now,' 'that's good, so can I hold him?' 'Sure,' as she handed me our son. While holding him I said a quick prayer thanking God for my son being born and being healthy and for me being there to witness. I held and kissed my son Cordial several time before leaving.

After leaving and once on the elevator to leave the hospital. I started thinking on how I really need to get my shit together. I'm a father now and it's not just about me anymore. I ended up getting a job with my sister at a Taco Bell in Livonia, Michigan. Once I started working my auntie never asked me for any money.

Chapter 43 'I Have Something For You'

Which allowed me to be able to save up enough money to be able to move. Into my own 1-bedroom apartment on Lasher near 8 mile Road. I stayed with my aunt for almost a year. Were her and her family treated me like I was one of them. She feed me and gave me a place to stay until I was able to get on my feet.

So, why some people may have whatever to say about my auntie, but I just know what she did for me, and I will be forever grateful to her and her family. I'm just hopeful that one day I'm able to repay her for the tremendous favor that I was given.

I moved into the same apartment complex that my sister lived with her mother. My apartment wasn't that far from my old neighborhood. I was working trying to fly straight but I didn't seem to have any money after paying most of my bills. So, I decided to get myself a second job. And I ended up getting a job on 8 mile at the Black Bunny warehouse. Where they mostly kept bread and some ice cream.

I was catching the bus to and from both jobs. I needed to get myself a car, so I managed to save up 500 dollars. And I gave my uncle Damon a call that was a car salesman. And I told him that I wanted to get a used car but I only had 500 dollars. And he said, 'let me see what I can do.' And after about a month my uncle called and asked, 'how much money do you have?' '500 dollars' 'okay I have something for you.'

The following weekend he called and told me 'come to the parking lot in the back' so I walked out there as he pulled up in a 1979 two door Burgundy Monti Carlo and got out of the car while saying 'what do you think?'

Chapter 44 A Half Ounce

'This is perfect, most of my friends are driving these old school cars.' 'It only has 70k miles and she only drove it to church and to the grocery store.' Now that I had a car, I needed to get some furniture. I had a bed that had been given and a stereo. So, I saved up a couple hundred and bought myself a used couch and matching loveseat.

Then one day while driving to work. I saw my boy that once hustled for me, so I pulled over and got out of the car in my uniform. 'What up doe Roc? What's up with that uniform?' 'I'm headed to work' and he started laughing 'are you for-real Bro?' 'Yeah, I'm working now,' as I laughed. 'If you ever want to get back to getting money just hit my up my number is still the same.' 'I got the same number also, but I need to get to work, so peace.'

After a few months of working both jobs. I'm still not making enough money so I beeped my boy. When he called back, I started explaining how I needed some work. And he asked, 'so what do you need Roc?' 'I'm thinking about a half but something that hasn't been stepped on much.' And I'm told 'just come through Roc,' so I went over to his house.

Once there I sat on the couch and we smoked a joint and played Madden. When the game was over, he got up and grabbed a half-ounce. I stood up to pay him and he said, 'your money isn't good with me this time Bra. If it wasn't for you looking out for me back then. I probably would be in jail or dead.' 'Are you sure?' 'I'm positive but if you need more just holler at your boy. And then I'll take your money.' And I walked out while saying 'good looking out I'll be hitting you up soon'

After completing my shift at work and once home. I put a pot of water on the stove to boil and I went to take a shower and change my clothes. When I returned to the kitchen the water was boiling and I placed the cocaine into a baby glass jar. Then I placed the jar into the pot and added baking soda and more things to help stretch the cocaine. Once I was done cooking the cocaine into crack. I almost had an ounce and I went and got a razor and begin cutting.

Chapter 45 Funny Money

The beige lump of crack into 10 dollar rocks. I didn't have any small baggies, so I used some weed baggies. Now I'm back to working and hustling again.

Then I got transferred to another Taco Bell, that was located in Ferndale, Michigan. After working there a few months I'm promoted to Shift Manager. That was cool but it didn't come with a pay increase. Then I heard about a guy that was selling counterfeit money. I didn't know him but I finally got in touch with the guy. And I bought 500 dollars' worth of counterfeit money for 75 dollars. I was really surprised at how real the money looked.

On the weekends and when I was off, I would go to several Adult Bars, and Fast Food restaurants. And I would order drinks or food with the funny money. Then I would put the change that I got back into my left pocket. I repeated that until I had no more funny money. I wanted to buy some more so I bought 5 thousand of funny money for 1500 hundred dollars. Then I took that funny money and bought 5 pounds of marijuana from an older caucasian guy. That grew it himself where he lived up in Northern Michigan. And he would come down to Detroit to sell his pounds to a guy I knew.

And around that same time, I hooked up with my cousin Lamar that produced easy listening music for himself. He started coming over to my apartment. And he had never created a hip hop track until we started working together. With his little QY10 drum machine and a very small Casio keyboard. It wasn't much but he was able to create tracks. Lamar would come over to my place and within a few months. He began producing tracks that I was eager to perform. After making a few tracks he said, 'you need something that can be played on the radio, Sergio. What your written is hot but there isn't any cursing on the radio. Write some lyrics for the radio, and I'll do the same with the music.' So, I took that as a challenge and I begin writing. And I'm using the same subject matter but not the same words.

The next time that he came over I had written a song with no cursing. So, after spitting the song that I wrote. 'That's what I'm talking about, Sergio that's dope and still hard'! With him doing my tracks now and no longer sampling records anymore. And if I wanted a baseline or some horns that I heard from a song. I would just let him hear it and he would play something similar.

We never drew up a contract it was just a simple 50/50 verbal agreement. I got 50% of the music and he got 50% of my lyrics. I would do my own management booking and promotion. And while performing I started noticing that my music was better than most of what was being performed. I was performing all over town. The Shelter, Saint Andrews, the Latin Quarters to name a few. I was starting to make a name for myself in the local hip hop community. And I'm still working and hustling as I'm trying to help provide for my son me and my bills.

Chapter 46 'Not Guilty I Want A Lawyer'

While weighing out some marijuana. I got a cellphone call from a female. That invited me to bring and sell her some marijuana for her party. After bagging up some marijuana for sale. I decided that I would stop by the party, make the quick sale for a quarter ounce then go visit a friend that lived in the area. When I came up off of the I 94 freeway while driving I made a wrong turn, so I went to turn back and I saw a police car. So, I slowed my speed as if I was looking for an address. I was hopeful that I didn't get pulled over because I'm driving dirty. And as I'm driving, I'm looking through my rear-view mirror. When I saw the police car make a U turn and now there behind me. Then shortly after I saw flashing red and blue lights, so I reluctantly pulled over. A police officer got out of his car and walked over towards my car. Once near my car he knocked on my window. I rolled down my window and put my hands on the steering wheel. Then he asked for my license and registration. I slowly reached into my pocket and grabbed my license. Then I told the police officer 'my registration is in my glove box,' as I'm told 'go ahead' as I slowly reached into my glove box to get my registration. I handed them both to the police officer and he walked back to his car to run my name.

When he returns, I'm asked to get out of the car please? I asked why? I'm told I have a bench warrant for your arrest, so I need for you to get out of the car.' I reluctantly got out of the car and after patting me down. I'm cuffed and escorted to the back seat of his police car. Once in the back seat of the officer's car he walked back to my car. And began searching through my car and he didn't find anything. Then he took my keys and opened up my trunk. I saw him moving things around then he pulled out a Mini Mack 10 Assault Rifle, that was behind my 12-inch kickers. Once I saw that I just dropped my head. Then the officer held up the gun and yelled 'what's this a squirrel gun?' Then I saw three more police cars arrive, and a tow truck pulled up to impound my car.The officer got back into the car and drove me to the precinct.

Once inside I had to go before another officer that's sitting behind a desk. I'm asked to empty my pockets so I took out everything but the marijuana. Then I'm told 'is that it, because I will search you?' So, I reluctantly pulled out the marijuana and dropped it onto the desk. He looked at the marijuana and said, 'that looks like a quarter ounce.' I looked at him surprised because it was. He must had notice me looking surprised because he said. 'I used to be a Detroit Officer for 15 years. And in Detroit this amount of weed wouldn't be anything but out here it's a lot.' Then I'm asked, 'what do you want to do about this?' 'I don't know' then he took the marijuana and said, 'don't worry about this,' as he tossed the marijuana into a nearby trash can. Then I'm escorted into a jail cell and once inside of the cell. I could hear what sounded like someone shoveling through the trash to retrieve the marijuana.

It's Thursday night and I won't be able to see a judge until Monday morning. I looked around the cell and I found an open cot. There was a payphone inside of the cell above my cot. Now I've been in a jail cells before but I've never seen a payphone inside of a cell.

Now it's Friday evening and the cell is starting to get full. While talking on the payphone I heard someone about to be placed into my cell. I saw an officer bringing a very drunk and short caucasian guy into the cell. And as the guy was being placed into the cell. He asked the officer 'can I make a telephone call?' The officer pointed at me and said, 'he looks white ask him,' as he slammed the cell closed. I'm laying down on the telephone when he loudly said, 'do I have to kick your ass to use the phone?' I told the girl that I was talking with to 'hold on,' as I set down the phone and I stood up. The little light weight guy then looked at my 6 foot 1 inch and 350-pound self and started stuttering. 'I'll just wait until you're done, sir, I'm sorry for bothering you.' Then he went over to the corner of the cell and sat on the floor because the cell was crowded. I got back on the telephone and was asked, 'what was that all about?' I told her about what just happen, as we laughed.

It was Saturday afternoon when an officer came into my cell and told me to come with him. I got up and he took me into an area to take my fingerprints. When he placed my fingers on the paper, I tried to roll my hand to prevent from getting a good print, but that didn't work because another officer saw what I was trying to do and he hit my hand and they got my fingerprints. Then an officer took me into a nearby office room. Where I'm told to have a seat, so I sat as the officer waited near the door.

After about 5 minutes the officer leaves, as two Federal Agents walked into the room. The one Federal Agent came over near me and started asking questions. 'What set do you claim?' 'What gang are you in?' 'Do you have any tattoos?' I answered no to all of his questions. Now I was wearing a black zipper hoodie with no shirt. The other Federal Agent walked over and opened up my hoodie and saw my surgical mark. And asked 'what's that?' as he pointed at my stomach. 'That's a surgical scar from being shot.' Then I asked, 'how come I haven't been read my rights?' And I'm told 'you don't have any fucking rights.' Then I said I want a lawyer.' And that's when he slammed a paper on the table in front of me and I looked at the paper and it was a list of my rights. And number six was the right to have a lawyer present. I was asked about the gun found in my car and I said 'thats not my gun I let someone use my car the other day.' After a while of trying to question me but not receiving any answers. I'm taken back into my cell.

Now it's Monday morning and I'm supposed to see a judge today. An officer came into my cell 'McGee,' as I stood up and he said, 'let's go,' as he put the handcuffs on me and escorted me to a police car in the parking lot. Where I was crammed into the back seat with two other people. And after a short ride I arrived at the courthouse on Kelly Road. The officer walked me into the courthouse, and I was told to have a seat in the pews, so I sat and waited. Once the judge called my name I walked up to the front. The judge read my charges and asked, 'how do you plea?' 'Not guilty and I want a lawyer.' The judge granted that I'm allowed to have a lawyer and I'm also released on a personal bond because I didn't have a criminal record. Once the judge said that I could go I just smiled at the officer that arrested me and he looked pissed. Another officer came over and took off the handcuffs and I walked outside of the courtroom.

Once in the lobby I used the payphone to call a friend. When she answered I asked her to come pick me up at the Harper Woods Court House. And to bring some money because I need to get my car out of the impound. Once she arrived, I got into the car and I told her 'I need to get my car that's in the impound so drive around the corner and then we'll switch spots. Once you have my car just meet me near the courthouse.' After switching cars, I drove to my apartment.

Once home I went straight into the bathroom and took a massive dump and a long hot shower. The next day I started looking through the Yellow Pages for a lawyer. Once I found a lawyer I called and after talking with him for a while he told me to come to his office.

Chapter 47 I Received A Notice

Once at his office on 6 Mile Road near Greenfield. We shook hands and he introduced himself again as Mr. Blacken . He told me to have a seat so I walked into his office and sat in a chair. We started discussing my case and I told him what I told the police and he interrupted me and said, 'I need for you to tell me the truth.' So, I told him a little more of the truth and he interrupted me again and said, 'look I need to know the whole truth not what you told the police. That way we both can tell the same lei if we have too.' Once he said that I told him the complete story. The gun was mine but I told the police that it wasn't. 'Now I can help you, so I need you to register for college classes. That way when you go before the judge. You can show that you're in school. Also, you need a piece of paper saying that you have a job. I don't care if it's a real job. But just a paper saying that you work.'

Once I left his office, I went straight up to WCCC and I registered for some classes. Then I went up to my uncle's alarm shop. Where I got a piece of paper saying that I worked there. Now that I had everything that I needed. I had to hit the streets to hustle up on some money I needed to pay for this lawyer.

Then after about 4 months I received a notice in the mail to appear at Wayne County Court. I became really excited when I learned that my case was being held in Wayne County. Because at that time I didn't know that Harper Woods was in Wayne County. When I arrived at the Frank Murphy Court House. I went through the metal detector and got onto the elevator.

Chapter 48 'What The Hell'

That took me to the 4th floor and my courtroom. While waiting in the hallway I saw my lawyer and he walked up to me. And he shook my hand and asked, 'did you get everything, Sergio?' 'I have everything,' 'that's good,' as we walked into the courtroom.

Once we entered my lawyer noticed the prosecutor and said, 'we went to law school together.' When my case was called, I walked up front and stood next to my lawyer. The judge told the prosecutor 'you may begin' as she stepped forward and said, 'we the people would like for the defendant to receive 15 years.' And I blurted out 'what the hell' and I'm told by the judge 'there will be no outburst in my courtroom, young man. Do you understand me?' 'Yes, I do.' Then my lawyer asked the judge 'could I speak with the prosecutor?' The judge granted and said, 'you have 5 minutes,' as he went to speak with the prosecutor. We're working out a deal and my lawyer notified the judge that they've reached a deal. Where I would have to meet with another judge. And that judge would decide if I qualified for their diversion program or prison.

Once outside of the courtroom my lawyer told me 'you're about to meet with that judge now. So, make sure you look him in the eyes and be sincere. This judge will decide on whether or not you go to prison, so if you have to act then act.' I walked down and around the hallway and I knocked on the door. And I'm told 'come in,' as I opened the door.

Once inside I'm told 'have a seat,' as I sat in the chair across from his desk. As I'm looking at the nameplate on his desk. The judge's name was Han Solo, so I assumed that he's a huge Star Wars fan. After answering several questions. He decided that I qualified for the program. So, I ended up getting 100 hours of community service. Along with 3 years of probation and I had to meet once a month with my probation officer. Where I had to take a drug test every month. And if I stayed out of trouble, I would be able to get my fingerprints back in five years. I was very happy to get the program and not prison and whenever I had a performance that was out of state. I would have to get a letter from my probation officer before I could leave.

While hustling to get money to pay off my lawyer. My beeper vibrates so I called the number back and it's my boy and he asked, 'do you want to do a song for a movie soundtrack'? 'Hell, yeah if you're serious.' 'I'm at the recording studio now. And the producer wants a verse added to the song and he asked if I knew anyone and I thought of you, so do you want to do this?' 'I'm in Highland Park right now?' 'It's either a yes or a no Roc because I can try to call someone else.' 'Just tell him I'll be there in less than an hour'.

Chapter 49 About My Promise

I got to Sound Suite Recording Studios on Puritan Avenue in about 45 minutes. Once buzzed in I told my boy 'good looking,' as he showed me to Studio A. While walking back to the studio I could hear the track playing. When I entered into the room the producer stood up and introduced himself and we shook hands. And he said, 'I need for you to write a verse to this,' as he played the track. I asked him about the movie and he started explaining the movie "Mirror Mirror'. I asked him to turn up the track as I started writing. After about an hour I was done so he asked to hear what I had wrote. I asked him to turn down the track and I started spitting what I wrote. He loved what I wrote and asked me to go into the booth and lay it to the track. I went into the booth and did my verse in one take. When I came back, he said, 'wow that was amazing'! And I asked, 'what was amazing?' 'How you just wrote that and did your verse in one take.' And I started laughing and said, 'this is what I do, so was that it?' 'That it,' so I gather my things and walked out of the Studio. But I was upset with myself after the fact for never signing any paper work or getting paid. I never even got a copy of the song on the soundtrack. Although I was told they used my verse but I don't know if that's true. I was so worried about getting back to getting money. So, that's my fault but in life you live and you learn, so that time I learned the hard way.

Once back at my apartment I went over to my sister's apartment. And I told her about what I had just done. 'That's great, Sergio, but you're still hustling right?' I was shocked at her response but not surprised. Then she started telling me 'you need to stop hustling your a father now, Sergio. You could get a job or go back to school you're not dumb. I mean anything but selling drugs.' At first, I couldn't argue because she was right. And I told her 'I don't want to hustle but I make more money than I do working both of my jobs.' 'That maybe true, Sergio but you already know there's no future in hustling. It's either prison or the grave, so do you want your son without a father?' 'You already know I don't want that why you think I'm busting my ass working two jobs?' She had me promise her that I would stop hustling. And I said, 'I'll quite hustling but not right now' and I walked out of her apartment.

Once at my apartment I'm still thinking about my promise. Then I changed my clothes and went to the spot in Highland Park. Now a spot is a house that you used to sell drugs from but it wasn't my spot. I would come through a lot and slang. I didn't want people to know that I was hustling. And most people including the police just assumed that I was just some caucasian teenager. That lived in the suburbs and wanted to be cool and buy drugs. Not knowing that I was the one selling the drugs. I had to learn how to use the way I looked to my advantage. I always wanted to keep a low profile. I never wanted to draw any unwanted attention. But there were times when people would try me and I would have to fight.

While knowing that most of the other hustlers were packing heat, so I decided to get myself a gun. I paid around 350 dollars for 9 millimeter but I've always believed if you pull out a gun, you better use that gun. Because I've been shot, so I'm not going through that shit again. I was out there hustling scared because I got too much to lose. I have a son now, so I have to hustle smatter.

An older guy once told me 'you need to learn the law if you're going to break the law.' So, I started reading and learning, as much as possible about what the police could and couldn't do by law. And the more I read the more I learned. So, I started transporting my drugs through cabs instead of my car that way. If ever stopped in a cab I could always claim that it wasn't mine.

Chapter 50 'Hold Up Anthony'

I started using ATM machines to move money around. Instead of having large amounts of money on me, so if I knew that I had to give someone some money. I would give them a debit card and have them withdraw the money when needed. I always kept a job and check stubs on me, so if the police ever pulled me over. I had check stubs as proof of me having a job. And that would explain me having money and by law they couldn't take my money although some did.

Around this time my mother had moved out with my brothers. And I didn't know where too. And I started dating a hostess at one of the restaurants I worked at named Nichole. And one evening I went over to Nichole's house to pick her up for a concert. When I arrived at Nichole's house. Her mother came to the door to let me in and said, 'Nichole is still getting ready so just have a seat in the Den,' as I walked into the Den. Her mother came into the Den and sat in a recliner. And that wasn't my first time being over her house or meeting her parents. Her mother started speaking with me about her job, as a teacher. Then I asked her 'is there a way to know what school a child is attending just by knowing their name?' And I'm told 'the child's name could be entered into a computer like we have at work. And the computer would give you the name of the school and the address that's used to register.' Once she said that I just told her 'my mother and brothers have moved but I don't know where too, and I'm just concerned.' Then she asked, 'why, Sergio'? 'I really don't know but I just want to know that there safe.' She stood up and walked over to their desk and grabbed a pin and paper. Then she handed them to me and asked me to write their names and when she gets to work on Monday. She'll enter their names into the computer and I'll see what I can find out, so just call me Monday afternoon. 'Thank you so much this really means a lot.' 'You're welcome but you can't tell anyone I'm not supposed to be doing this.' 'I won't,' as Nichole walked into the Den. And said, 'I'm ready now,' as we walked out of the house. Once in my car as I started driving towards Cobo Hall in Downtown Detroit. After parking and making it to our seats. I enjoyed my very first concert "Anita & Luther."

And on Monday afternoon I called Nichole's house. Her mother answered the telephone and said, 'hello, Sergio I have some information but remember no one must know.' 'I won't even tell Nichole,' as I'm given the name of the school and the address that was used, as I wrote the information down. 'Thank you, so much.' 'You're more than welcome, Sergio. I hope that you're able to find your family.' 'Thank you again and me too.' 'I'm going to let Nichole know that you're on the telephone,' as she set the telephone down. Once Nichole got onto the telephone. We spoke for a while but I'm still thinking about my family.

Once off the telephone I started looking at the information. And I'm thinking that I finally may know the whereabouts of my family. I was already in the process of moving in with a female friend from high school and her grandmother. When I called an older friend named Anthony, that lived around the corner. When he answered I asked, 'could I get a ride to where my family maybe?' 'Sure, just give me about thirty minutes and I'll be around there.' I called him because he drove a Station Wagon at that time. And if I needed to bring them and their things back with me, I would have the room. Once I heard him blow the horn. I rushed downstairs and jumped into the car, as I gave him the address. And we drove onto Keystone Street on the EastSide of Detroit near Nevada.

Once at the address as I'm looking for any signs of my family. I asked Anthony to park a few houses down, as he drove back some. I'm really nervous, as I slowly got out of the car and walked towards the house. Once on the porch I started knocking. I'm grasping my gun in my pocket just in case there's an unruly boyfriend. After knocking a little louder my mother finally came to and cracked the door. And I said, 'you can't open the door up mom?' And she opened the door a little more as she looked surprised to see me. She also appeared to be half the size that I remembered. After asking to be let into the house several times as she just stood there and said nothing. Out of frustration I just forced my way into the house, as she stumbled back.

Once in the living room I'm looking around and the house looked like a drug spot. There's hardly any furniture and I looked into the dining room. Where I saw a large whole in the ceiling. Then she asked, 'why are you hear, Sergio?' 'I didn't know where y'all were, so I had to find you guys.' I'm assuming my brothers heard me because they ran up and started hugging on me. My youngest brother Michael told me how he didn't like being there or that man that's with our mother. And I told him 'go get y'all stuff y'all coming with me,' as they went back into their bedroom to get their things. Then they came back out with garbage bags and I told them 'go put your things in Anthony car outside,' as they walked out of the house. I noticed that my mother hadn't moved. So, I asked, 'how come you're not getting your stuff mom?' 'I'm not leaving,' as two of my brothers came back into the house. And I told them 'go get mom stuff and put it into the car for me please,' as they went to grab her things. She still hadn't moved, so I looked at my mother and told her 'you're going to leave even if I have to carry your ass out of here.' And that's when she reluctantly got up and started walking out of the house. And I noticed while she was walking that she was limping.

Once everything and everyone was in the car and Anthony was about to pull off. My brother Michael said, 'that's the man that hurt mommy's leg,' as he pointed up the street. And I said, 'hold up Anthony,' as he parked the car. And my mother yelled 'just drive off, Sergio' . Now I'm really pissed, so that explained why she's limping. I looked and the guy was up the street but was walking towards the car. Once he got closer to the car I got out of the car and I approached him and asked, 'you got a cigarette'? Even though I don't smoke but I wanted to get closer to him. He patted his pockets, as he was looking for his cigarettes. And I'm assuming that he heard or saw my family, as he turned to run so I punched him and he fell into the middle of street. I stood over him and I pulled out my gun.

Chapter 51 'What Did They Do Now?'

'So, you're the one that jumped on my mother. We'll fight with me you punk bitch,' as I punched him several times. I could hear my mother screaming very loudly while I was punching him, so I thought she had gotten out of the car. When I turned towards the car to see if my mother got out the car. The guy got up and ran between some houses. I started to shoot at him but I'm in the middle of the street and its broad daylight and Anthony screamed 'let's go Roc before the police come.' I reluctantly got back into the car and we drove off.

Once back on the WestSide of Detroit. I had to find somewhere for my family to stay because I'm no longer staying at the house on Curtis. So, my family ended up staying at a shelter that was near where I was staying on San Juan Street near Puritan Avenue.

After about a month or so in the shelter. My mother found and got a house for rent that was a few streets over from where I was staying. After a while I decided to move in with them. I'm still dating an attractive young lady named Tamil. That I meet and started dating while in my apartment. Then after a while Tamil told me that she was pregnant. I was shocked but not surprised because it wasn't like I was using any protection. And I already had my son Cordial with another woman, so now I'm about to be a father again. I'm 23 and I'm about to have two children, so I really needed to get my shit together.

After six months Tamil gave birth to our son Denzel. Now I have two children with two women and I'm dating another attractive young lady named Marie. Then I got a telephone call from Tamil and she told me that she wasn't getting along with her mother, and how she wanted to leave. After talking with her for a while I told her 'just come and stay with me.' Then shortly after Tamil moved into my mother's house in the basement with me. I really liked having Tamil there because I got to see my son Denzel every day and I didn't have to get a room whenever we had sex.

Then after a performance I meet with a few of the guys. That once was signed to Golden Records. And there telling me about this new record label there on and how I should come and get down. 'I'm not sure I'm tired of the false promises.' And while at another performance I ran into some more guys and the same thing 'come get down with us IROC.'

After several months of recording and performing I decided to call one of the guys, that I saw while performing. And I told him 'I want to check out Bullet Records. I'm told 'no doubt Roc just meet me on 7 mile and Greenfield in an hour.'

Once there I followed him to Bullet Records on 6 miles across Woodward. When we both pulled up into the back of the house. I got out of the car and he said, 'follow me,' as we walked into the house. Once inside I saw several people that use to be on Golden Records. After catching up with the guys. I asked, 'where is the Executive Producer?' I'm told he's upstairs and I'm shown the stairs.

Chapter 52 Michigan State Fair

Once I got up there, I saw how he had transformed. The whole upstairs into a recording studio and sound booth. There's a guy sitting in front of the mixing board. Then he stood up and walked over and introduced himself, as Big E. We shook hands, as I told him that I'm IROC and he said, 'have a seat,' as we both sat in front of the mixing board. 'I've been hearing a lot of good things about you.' And I said, 'you can't believe everything that you hear' and he said, 'that's so true, so do you have any of your music?' 'Yeah, I got a couple of my cassettes,' as I handed them to him. He placed one of my cassettes into the player and my music started playing. He's bobbing his head and then he turned the volume up while saying 'that's dope' and he listen to three more songs. Then said, 'that shit should be on the radio right now.' And he asked, 'who's doing your tracks?' I told him 'me and my cousin,' as he forward to the next song.

After listening to a few more songs. He turned off the music and said, 'I've heard enough everything that I've heard was dope, so I don't need to hear any more!' 'I really want you on my label, so what do you think?' 'I would have to think about that, but if I did sign, I must have creative control over my music and shows. Also, only me and my cousin can produce my tracks.' 'That's fine I wouldn't want anyone else after hearing what I've heard.' And after about a month or so I got with Bullet Records. I never signed a contract or anything and I spent several years on Bullet Records. I did everything that I was asked to do, as did Bullet Records.

Now I've done several performances over the years with that label in and out of town but the biggest local performance to me was at the Michigan State Fair. Where I along with another Artist on Bullet Records were to perform. There was a soundcheck a few hours before the show. Once I arrived in a stretched limo owned by Bullet Records. I summited my music to the soundcheck guy. And after a few minutes, I performed my song on stage. After getting my levels for my music and microphone situated. Once finished I headed back to Bullet Records studio and waited.

Then around 7 pm I arrived back at the State Fairgrounds. And as I'm riding through the parking lot, I saw thousands of people that were already out there, as there breaking through barriers in front of the police. It looked like a Michael Jackson concert was about to take place. It was so packed that it literally took us about ten minutes or more just to drive about fifty yards to the back of the Band Shell Stage.

Once out of the car I walked onto the back of the Band Shell Stage. Then I walked through a small hallway that lead out to the stage. I just wanted to see the crowd size, so I peaked. And it was getting closer to show time when Bone Thugs in Harmony arrived. I always got butterflies in my stomach before performing. But I became even more nervous after I peeked again, and the crowed size was massive. I'm thinking there were about twenty thousand people or more. After several acts had performed it was show time for me, so I walked onto the stage during my intro.

Chapter 53 I Was Violated

Once my music dropped, I began doing my thang. While performing I notice that Tamil was in the crowd and she's near the front of the stage. The crowd started pushing forward so I pointed to someone on stage. And once I got his attention I waved until he knew to make sure that Tamil would be safe. After my set I went backstage and I'm sweating. And I could hear the crowded screaming whistling and clapping. And that really felt great because to me it was conformation that I gave them a good performance.

Then later that year I was in Bullet Records Recording Studio on Christmas Eve. My cousin Lamar had produced me a track. And once done he leaves, but I decided to stay, and I produced myself another track. And I'm smoking and drinking now that Lamar was gone because he doesn't smoke, or drink and I didn't want to indulge while he was there. Once everything that I had created was saved. I was still feeling it, so I decided to smoke and drink some more. And I started messing around with the keyboard. And within a few hours I had produced a R&B slow track. And I had never made a R&B track before, but I'm really feeling the track. So, after listening and smoking to the track for a while. I decided to write some lyrics. I had never written a slow song or anything else other than hip hop. But I figured it couldn't be that difficult, so I rolled up another blunt and started writing.

Once done I had produced and wrote a slow song that I titled "Nothing But A Love Thang." That Bullet Records released on a compilation album that was titled 'Front Street.' Once done it was really late around 4am or later. When I decided to drive home and it's probably five inches of snow on the ground and it's snowing. I'm super blowed and I barely made it home.

Once at the house I quietly unlocked the door to the basement. And I started walking down the blurred stairs and I'm trying to remain quiet. I knew that Tamil was asleep and as I'm walking across the floor. I tripped over something and Tamil awoke. After apologizing for waking her up as I sat at the foot of my bed. And I started talking with Tamil and I just passed out.

Several hours later I woke up and I'm in the bed and I'm covered. So, I pulled the cover back and I noticed that I'm nude and my penis was sticky, as if I had sex. So, I nudged Tamil and when she woke up I asked, 'what happened last night?' 'You got undressed and jumped my bones'! Now I don't believe that happen. I passed out at the foot of the bed and I think I was violated that night. I believe Tamil had her way with me and a few months later I'm told that she's pregnant. And at that time, I'm only hustling and with me being in and out of the house a lot between hustling, recording and performing. I decide to put a Padlock on the basement door.

Then one day while at the Studio recording and Tamil was at work. I came home and I noticed that the screws to the lock had been rescued, so after unlocking the door. I went down into the basement.

Chapter 54 I Was There About 3 Weeks

While looking around to see if anything was missing. I noticed that all of Tamil's jewelry had been taken. Including her high school class ring. I stormed back upstairs and barged into my brother's bedroom and yelled 'who the hell broke into the basement?' As they claimed not too, so I started whooping their asses with my fist. And my mother heard me beating them, so she came to the doorway and asked, 'what did they do now?' I told her about what they had done, and she screamed 'but isn't that enough, Sergio there bleeding?' I said, 'they should be glad that it isn't worse,' as I stumped back into the basement.

Once seated on my bed. I'm thinking about how I tell Tamil. And when she came into the basement. I just told her about what happened and she begin to cry. And not long after Tamil moved back in with her mother. And I couldn't blame her if I could afford to move. I would've. A few months later I went to get into my car. And as I hit my alarm remote but it didn't chirp, so I thought my battery was bad. So, I looked under my car hood and I saw that my battery had been stolen. I went straight into my brothers' bedroom and I started beating them silly. I found out that they exchanged my battery for a few used video games at a store around the corner.

The next morning, I started looking through the newspaper for a house to rent. This was years before the internet and I found a house that I could afford. But I was very apprehensive about getting that house at first because the house was located on Washburn. The same street where I had been shot but this house was near School-craft Street, so I called and got the house. I moved into the house and Tamil moved in with me. I was there about 3 weeks before my mother lost her house, and they moved in also. Now I'm trying to manage the drama between my mother brothers, and a pregnant Tamil.

Chapter 55 Yard Conversation

After several months' Tamil was about to give birth. And she's trying to do whatever she could to go into labor. And I believe my friend Stan's girlfriend at that time told her about taking some castor oil and a warm bath. And by doing that she could help to induce her labor. Once I was home and within a couple of hours of Tamil taking a bath. I had to rush Tamil to the hospital where I witnessed her give birth to our beautiful daughter Nichole. I had never seen a childbirth before, and I saw parts of Tamil that she will never see. Now I'm a father of three children with two different women, and I'm still dating Marie.

After a few weeks of Nichole's birth. I decided that I would tell Marie about my daughter, but I didn't know how to tell her that I've had a child with another women while we were dating. So, one evening when Marie came over to the house while Tamil was at work. I got into her car and I decided to just come out and tell her. And I said what I said and she was pissed. Then shortly after that I didn't speak or date Marie anymore. I knew that I had mess things up and I only had myself to blame. And not too long after that happened. Me and Tamil moved out of my house on Washburn and into a house that her mother owned.

The house was located on Biltmore Street near 7 mile. I no longer had a car, so I would use Tamil's car a red 4 door Ford Escort, that her mother had bought for her before getting her a job at Ford Motor Company with her. Now at that time I'm not working and I'm only hustling and my hustle was really slow. And we would argue a lot about me not contributing towards the bills. I wasn't working so I figured I would do whatever else that I could do around the house. My thought was I may not be able to buy the diapers but I could change them. I would look after our children whenever Tamil had to work. Then one day Tamil told me that her mother had threatened to take away her car if she ever heard that I drove her car again. And that caused even more arguments, but I still drove just not as much. After looking for a job for several months in the newspapers. I finally got a job through a temp service.

Then one day while I was outside doing some yard work in the front yard. My oldest son Cordial grandfather walked up, but I didn't recognize him. Then he asked, 'aren't you, Sergio?' 'I am, why?' Then he said 'you need to see and spend more time with your son Cordial ' I couldn't say anything because he was right. 'I live right down the street from you,' as he pointed. 'You could come down there anytime to see your son.' And I asked, 'does my son live there?' 'No, he doesn't but he's there all of the time. And here take my telephone number,' as he handed me a piece of paper. Then he asked, 'are you working, Sergio?' And I told him 'I have a temp job right now, but I'm still looking.' Then he told me go downtown to the Meat Factory and tell them that I sent you,' as he walked away.

I went and applied and got that job at the Meat Factory. The first day they had me cleaning chitlins, so I ended up quitting after only working two days. And unfortunately, shortly after that yard conversation. My son's grandfather passed away in a motorcycle accident. While I'm sad for their lost I'm also happy that Renee, and my oldest son will be moving into his home down the street.

Chapter 56 It's Only Been A Week

Then later that year we threw our daughter Nichole a birthday party in our backyard. We had invited a bunch of other children including my oldest son and his mother. I was pleasantly surprised once they arrived. I was on the bbq grill as I'm looking, and the mothers of my children are talking. And they appeared to be getting along. I was really happy to have all of my children together.

Then after that birthday party. The house that Tamil grew up in became available. And she kept mentioning how she would rather have that house then the house we're in, so I told Tamil 'just asked your mother for the house if it means that much to you'. 'She's not just going to give me that house, Sergio. She would rather sell me the house.' 'Then offer to buy the house.' I'm assuming that she took my advice because a few weeks later. Tamil told me that she agreed to sell her the house for 50 thousand dollars'. And we ended up going to a Mortgage Company in Birmingham, Michigan. Where Tamil applied and was approved for a home loan.

After about a month or so, we got the three bedroom brick bungalow on Rosemont Street between Outer Drive and 7 mile Road. Once we got the keys. We entered into the house and the house was trashed. With garbage and clothes all throughout the house. There's also multiple colors of carpet on the floors. So, the next day we went over and removed all of the trash and clothes. The house needed a lot of work. And the multi colored carpet needed to be pulled and the walls needed to be painted. Once I got the carpet pulled, I noticed the floors needed to be sanded. And one of the back bedrooms had paneling that had been glued to the wall. So, after removing the paneling I saw several holes in the walls, so I patched the holes. Then we walked throughout the house and she made out a huge list of things that needed to be done. I thought Tamil would be helping so the list didn't seem too big. But what I didn't know was that I would be doing all of the work by myself. And whenever she would bring people over to show them the house. She would always tell them how we did this, and we did that,' but we haven't done crap. Other than making a few trips to Home Depot to get more supplies for me. I ended up given my brothers a few dollars to help expedite the finishing of the house. I worked for three weeks in a role on that house. After work and on weekends until the house was moved in ready.

And within a year after moving into that house. I manage to save up 1,000 dollars to get myself a used car. So, I started looking through newspapers. And after visiting several used car lots. I found and bought a four door Grey Ford Taurus. Now that I had my own transportation, I decided to get myself a second job.

I got a job at an Italian restaurant in Plymouth, Michigan as a dishwasher. After several months I became a Sauté Cook, then a Line Cook. I was making a little more money, so I decided to quit working at the temp job. Then my friend Stan came over to the house and he started telling me about a "hook up" on getting a job with the big 3. He told me about how a guy that was doing some work at his father's house mentioned 'I could get you into the big 3 if you want.' Stan told me the guy worked with or for Ford Motor Company Union. 'And I have the same name as my father, so we should go up there."

After convincing me to go we arrived at the Trenton Plant Union Office. Where we meet with the guy and after shaking hands and introducing ourself. He asked, 'would you guys like to work for Ford or one of the big 3?' And we both said that we would. He said, 'okay then just fill out this paperwork,' as he placed some papers in front of us and said, 'I'll see what I can do.' So, we filled out the paperwork all the while not knowing if we're going to get a job.

Now that happened in March of 1999 and we both received a call to take a drug test in April of that same year. I stopped smoking marijuana and took some supplements to help cleanse my systems. I took the drug test a week later and I was really nervous about the result because it's only been a week. After taken the test I'm told that I passed and I was given a business card with a number to call.

Once home I called the number and it was a recording telling me the time date and place to take a test. After that I called Stan and told him about my call and he told me that he got the same message.

The following week I drove to the address to take my test. Once inside I saw Stan and about 25 other people or more. We were put into groups and my group was instructed to go into a room. And once inside of the room that's set up like a classroom where I took a test. And once done I'm told there's another test and it ended up being a three part test. A written mechanical and verbal. It took me two days and about five hours each day to complete all of the test. Once done I wasn't told if I had passed or not. I was just told that I'll be notified by mail. And after a few weeks of waiting I received a letter from Chrysler in the mail.

Chapter 57 Congratulations

When I opened the letter, it read 'Welcome to the Chrysler Corporation.' With the place date and time to report. I was really excited when I learned that I finally had a real job with benefits and health insurance. I called Stan to tell him about my letter. And that I'm to report to the Detroit Axle Plant. And he told me 'I got a letter also to report to the Jefferson North Plant.' Once I arrived at the mammoth Detroit Axle Plant that was on Linch Road near Van Dyke, on the EastSide of Detroit. Once inside I'm taking into an office, we're I went through their orientation process. After completing orientation I'm told I'll be part time at first. And after my ninety day probation I would be considered for full time employment. I'm told that I can't miss any days or call off during my probation. And I'll only be working on Mondays, Fridays and Saturdays.

Once inside of the plant I'm giving a pair of earplugs and safety glasses. Then I'm walked through the plant to an assembly line that's near the back of the plant. Where I'm shown how to perform several jobs. And I'm shown how to perform several jobs because with being part time. I may have to do any one of these jobs.

On my first day I was giving a pretty easy job but the next day I was doing the job that no one wanted. The assembly line that I started on built axles for cars, and trucks. That job was really oily and dirty and it was located at the end of the assembly line. Where I had to place a brake boot onto the axle, as it came down the line. I only had a few seconds to place the boot onto the axle. And every day I was placed on that same job. So, after a while I just started going to that job automatically. I already knew that's where I would be placed. I became so good at doing that job that even my supervisor often would come up to me and say, 'you're doing this job a lot better than anyone else.' After a while I developed a routine on how to do that job. The brake boots that I had to place on the axle would be on a spindle wrapped in plastic behind me. And I would have to cut the plastic with a box cutter.

Then grab a boot and place it onto the axle. I became so good at that job that I would walk up the assembly line. While talking shit with my coworkers and make it back in time to put the boot onto the axle within seconds.

After 13 months of not missing a day or being late I'm told 'congratulations you'll be full time on Monday.' I was so excited to learn that I'll be full time because it wasn't easy. I knew several people that started when I did and they didn't make it through their probation.

Chapter 58 'The Production Will Drop'

On Monday, I went to the end of the assembly line. Where I would put on brake boots for several years. Then I heard there was an opening in the Hammer Hole. The Hammer Hole was a separate department, that's near the assembly line. The Hammer Hole was where the bolts got pressed into the axle's tubes. The tube were placed onto a carousel that took the tubes over to the supper-finisher station. Then after being supper finished the tubes were placed onto another carousel. That took the tubes down to the assembly line.

Once I got the job my first job there was a loader. We're I would take two tubes out of two metal bens that's behind me and I would place them onto a conveyer that was in front of me to be pressed. Were another person that stood next to me would place the bolts into the axle tubes. Then the conveyer would take the tubes into a machine were the bolts would get pressed into the axle tubes. Once the tubes came out of the machine another person across from me would pick up the tube and place it onto the carousel. That took the tubes over to the Supper finisher station. Were a person would take two tubes and place them into the Supper finisher machine. Once done the Supper finisher would place the tubes onto a carousel that would head down towards the assembly line. Where someone would grab an axle tube and place it inside of the axle.

After a few years of doing the unloading job. I became a Supper finisher and I liked that job because it was a two man job. I would work for thirty minutes on and thirty minutes off. The lightest tube that I handled weighed about twelve pounds and the heaviest about twenty seven pounds. After grabbing two tubes at a time for thirty minutes. Those tubes would seem to get heavier and I did that job for several years, as I keep complaining about the old (GreenField Village) equipment, that were using to get our production. Our production number at that time was 1000 parts per shift. But we would be lucky to get 700 pieces.

After several years of complaining. They finally built a new computerized Hammer Hole. And there was a merger, so I was told it's no longer Chrysler, but Daimler Chrysler.' My supervisor asked if I wanted to become a job setter of the new Hamer Hole. I told him that I would like to become a job setter, so he arranged for me to be trained. I was taught how to perform minor repairs and if there was a major problem that I couldn't manage. I was told to radio for skill trades.

Once the new Hammer Hole was up and running. I asked my supervisor 'what's our production number now?' He told me 'the new number will be 2,000 parts per shift.' And we argued about that number and then he said, 'whenever you guys get that number y'all can stop working and still get paid.' 'Are you sure?' 'Yes, I am.' The first day we only got 1,300 parts that shift. Then after telling the crew what the supervisor said. They started working even harder trying to get that production number. Other than making minor repairs I also would relieve people, so they could use the restroom. I decided that I would start helping them with their work. And within a week we had created a working routine. And we started getting our production number. Then we started getting over the production number in five hours.

The supervisor couldn't believe our production numbers and asked. 'How are y'all doing this?' 'It's just good hard teamwork, but don't forget your promise because the minute you renege on your word the production will drop back down.' And after a few weeks of over production he went back on his word, so our production dropped. And after a few days of low production, he called me into his office and said, 'you guys will get paid again if you get production and leave.' And I reminded him 'if you go back on your word again the production will drop again.' 'I know I know.' The next day we got 2,300 parts in five hours and it was on a Friday night and I had a performance, so I left.

After a few years of living as if I was married. I decided that I should get married to the mother of my two youngest children. I had a good job with benefits and I wasn't hustling or smoking anymore. It just seemed to be the next logical progression. I purchased a not so expensive ring and I proposed.

Chapter 59 'I Physically Cant'

Tamil said yes so, we took over a year to plan and pay for everything. I didn't want a big wedding but Tamil did, so after compromising we agreed on 250 people. Which I thought was still too many. Tamil wanted a church wedding, but I was content with just going to a Justice of the Peace. My mother and auntie Marie were already attending a Baptist church that wasn't to far from our house, so we started attending that church several months before our wedding date. After a service I asked the pastor if I could get married at the church? I was told that I could but since I wasn't a member. I would have to pay $50 and attend marriage counseling. I agreed and asked, 'when do we come for counseling?' 'A few weeks or a month before the wedding.'

A month before the wedding we meet with the pastor in his office. Once seated the pastor started asking us several questions. And I started realizing that our answers to his questions wasn't on the same page. And I started feeling that I shouldn't be getting married but I chose to ignore my apprehension.

Tamil wanted to have her dress made and I told her that I think that would cost a lot more compared to just buying a dress.' But she was adamant on getting her dress made, so she had it made.

At that time, she was doing all of the wedding planning. And after several months of her complaining and getting frustrated. I told her that I would help with the planning. Once involved in the planning I realized how much this wedding was costing. I couldn't believe that the cost was already at 10k, and she's still adding more things. I'm already working five or six days a week and most of those days I'm doing sixteen hour shifts. I saw that I wasn't making enough money to help pay for this over the top wedding.

So, I ended up getting a second job as a janitor. At a Paint Factory in Pontiac, Michigan. My second job was five days a week and forty plus hours. After being involved in planning for a while. I told her that I can't work any more hours than I am now. The wedding cost had gotten to 14k, so I told her 'we should just go to Toledo and get married and save this money,' but she wanted to get married in a church. I told her that 'we need to save some money,' so I suggested that we should go to Chicago to purchase the liquor for the open bar at the reception because it's a lot cheaper. And she agreed, so the following weekend we drove to Chicago to purchase the liquor. We got several half gallons at a drive-through liquor store. After purchasing the liquor, we drove through an Elvis themed McDonalds to get something to eat.

The following weekend we went up to the VFW Hall that would be hosting our reception on 10 mile in Southfield, Michigan. The Hall offered a catering package that included a bartender, so we purchased that package and paid for the Hall. And I believe we spent sixteen dollars per plate. My sister paid to have the Hall decorated with balloon arches and balloons throughout the Hall.

And Tamil keep adding to the cost of the wedding and after seeing the amount reach over 20k I just stop counting. I'm already averaging eighty plus hours a week at Chrysler and I'm working forty plus hours a week at my second job. And I told her 'you can't keep adding things to this wedding. It's costing us too much money already I physically can't work any more hours than I am now.'

So, for our reception we made our own table favors. I had never been to both a wedding and reception before. I usually only went to the receptions, so I didn't have an example of how a wedding should look. Then she rented two old school limos that picked up both wedding parties and took us to the church. I got dressed at my house and I helped my youngest son Denzel get dressed. After my Groomsman arrived including my oldest son Cordial. We got into the limo and headed towards the church. And my children were in my wedding. My daughter Nichole was the flower girl. And my youngest son Denzel was the ring barrier. My oldest son Cordial stood next to my Groomsmen. And during the wedding, as I'm standing at the alter waiting on Tamil to walk down the aisle. After the I do's I remember taken a bunch of pictures and getting into the limousine and heading to the reception hall.

Chapter 60 Once The Reception

Once both wedding parties arrived at the reception Hall. We got out of the limos and lined up outside of the Hall. Then we walked into the Hall, as were being announced. And once inside the wedding party was escorted to our seats at two beautifully dressed long tables, that was located on the south-side of the Hall. Once seated I'm facing the guest, that's seated at several round tables in front of me. There was a small stage that was located across the hall from me and an open Bar that was located on my right that was near the front door. My friend from 1st Class, that was deejaying on the local radio station. I asked and he agreed to deejay my reception and he was setup on the small stage. As I was looking onto the guest, I saw Renee, my oldest son's mother and her older sister seated. Then I was really surprised when I looked and saw my father, so I quickly waved for my friend and bodyguard Big Deal to come over to my table. Once he came as I pointed towards my father and said, 'if he gets drunk and starts acting a fool, I want you to quickly throw his ass out of here please.' 'Okay Roc.'

After everyone ate and Tamil and I danced with each other's parents. After partying for a while I was summoned to the middle of the dance floor. Once there I saw Tamil sitting in a folded chair and I was told to take Tamil garter off with my teeth, so I reluctantly got down on my hands and knees. And I crawled towards Tamil and I used my teeth to remove her garter.

After partying some more I walked over to the cake table with Tamil. And she cut a piece of the wedding cake. The wedding cakes were beautiful and I say cakes because there were seven cakes. The cakes were connected by bridges and on the top of the bridges. There were twelve plastic people toppers that represented the twelve members of the wedding party. There was some kind of water feature at the center of the cakes. That I thought was beautiful but a bit too much.

Then after several hours of partying we walked over to the gift table as we looked at a few of the gifts. Then we went over to another table where we had a Wishing Well, that we rented. That was filled with several envelopes' of cards and money.

Once the reception came to an end we got a ride to the Holiday Inn. That was located around the corner on Telegraph road. And once inside of our room we put our gifts and cards onto the bed. Then I dumped the Wishing Well onto the bed as many envelopes just poured out.

Chapter 61 After 10 days

The next morning, we got dressed and grabbed our luggage. And headed towards her car that had been dropped off the day before. Once inside we drove to Detroit Metro Airport. Where we boarded an airplane and flew to Orlando Florida.

Once in Orlando we got onto a shuttle that took us straight to the Disney Caribbean Resort. Where we were residing and the hotel looked like a condo. The room we had was beautiful and on top of the king-sized bed there was a "Welcome to the Caribbean" wicker basket. With several items for me and Tamil.

After changing our clothes we went outside and maybe fifty yards away. There was a white sanded beach that was beautiful. It looked like a picture on a postcard. We walked down towards the beach and I seen a huge man-made lake and a place near where you could rent boats. So, I decided to rent a boat and once on the boat I drove all around that lake. While on the boat we seen a private island, so once off of the boat. We decided to walk over onto a small bridge that was connected to the beach. When we walked over the bridge I looked down into the water and I seen several big turtles.

Once on the island we were able to walk around and explore. And there were a few small vending machines that sold animal feed. So, I purchased a few and feed the fishes and turtles. After being on the island for a while we decided to go back to our room and rest.

Then after a few hours, and changing our clothes again. We decided to go back out and in-front front of the hotel where there were several shuttle benches. Where the shuttles would arrive every twenty minutes. And the shuttles would have the name of the theme park that it would take you to on the front and side of the shuttle. We were only there for ten days so every day I would devise a plan of what we could do for that day. I remember doing a lot of walking at the theme parks. And I was trying to dress "fresh", so I brought some brand new gym shoes that I had never worn. And I ended up with two big blisters on both of my big toes. Other than that I really enjoyed myself.

After 10 days our honeymoon was over and once back home. I'm doing 90% of the cooking and 70% of the laundry and more than 50% of the house cleaning.

Chapter 62 'Let's Go'

I did all of the yard work while working seventy hours a week or more at Chrysler. I wouldn't get home from work until midnight or later. Then I would take a shower and go into the basement to unwind. I usually didn't go to bed until around two am, or later. Only to awake at six am to get my children up and ready for school by six thirty am.

Once I gathered them into the basement. I would fix them breakfast and help them with their homework if needed. One morning while I was fixing their breakfast. I noticed that my daughter hair wasn't done. So, I asked, 'what happened to your hair?' 'Mommy is to ruff so can you do my hair?' 'I don't know how baby girl, but I'll try.' And after attempting to do her hair for weeks. I eventually taught myself how to part braid and put her hair into ponytails.

Once ready for school I would drive them to school on 7 mile and Lasher. And whenever I had to meet with their teachers. I would come into the school for meetings. And I also would come into the school on my children's birthdays, and on holidays to bring treats for the whole classroom. A teacher once told me 'it's really refreshing to see a father that's so involved with their children's schooling. I hardly ever see their mother.' 'My wife works days and I work afternoons, so that's why you guys see me more.'

Then after dropping my children off at school. I would run around town paying bills and grocery shopping. Once done if I was lucky. I would take a short nap and my shift started at two thirty pm, but I would leave earlier. The plant was surrounded by railroad tracks, so I would get to work around two pm. And a few times I got caught waiting on a train to pass, but I never was late because I had left early enough. I had repeated that routine for several years.

Then on a Thursday night after getting home from work. I took my shower and eventually got into the bed. And while sleeping I had a vivid dream and in my dream, Tamil was at a Rams Horn type restaurant. And I just appeared at the door and I walked in and asked the Hostess 'where's my wife?' And the Hostess pointed me in her direction and I began walking towards where she was seating. Now she was sitting in a red booth with her best female friend. And I could tell there's two guys sitting with them but I wasn't able to see their faces. Once I walked up and stood there and I didn't say anything. Then when she looked up and seen me, she looked very shocked. Then I woke up and I sat up in the bed and I'm trying to make sense of my dream. And after a while I decided to wake up Tamil, so I nudged her and when she woke up. I started telling her about my dream and she had that same look on her face as in my dream. And she told me 'that's just a dream, Sergio. I'm not cheating on you, so go back to sleep' and she went back to sleep. But I couldn't I'm still sitting up trying to understand my dream.

Then a few weeks later I started noticing that she's coming home a lot later than usual. And she's also making a lot of excuses for being late, that wasn't making much sense. And we're also arguing a lot more so now I'm thinking something must be going on. Then maybe two months after my dream. She told me how we need to separate, and I told her 'I'm tired of arguing in front of the kids to but I don't think separating will fix that maybe we should try dating again,' and she agreed. And then said, 'but I still think that we should separate. And I really didn't understand her saying that because she had just agreed with me about trying to date again. Then I'm told 'I think one of us should move out of the house.' And I said, 'I don't think that's a good idea Tamil.' Then she said, 'if you don't want to move out Sergio then I will.' And I said, 'I don't think that's a good idea, but if you think that will help then I'll move. Because I don't want my children uprooted. And we need to tell our children.' So, we gathered the children into the basement. And once the children were seated, I began to explain. 'I'll be moving out for a while we're going to take a quick break, so we won't be arguing around you guys anymore.' And as I'm explaining to our children. I noticed that Tamil really hasn't said much and that seemed weird, because we both are supposed to be telling them.

Then the next month I started packing as I waited for my taxes to arrive. Once my taxes arrived, I moved into a 1 bedroom apartment in Westland, Michigan. We never went on a date in fact we only meet once. At a restaurant on Plymouth and Farmington. I arrived at the restaurant first and was waiting on Tamil. And when she walked in and before I could say anything. She said, 'I want a divorce' and I said, 'but what about what we told the children?' 'That what I want' and she started walking away and I said, 'so just like that?' And she turned back around and said, 'just like that' and walked out of the restaurant. I believe my dream was Gods way of telling me. That my wife was cheating. She filled for the divorce and because of us having two small children. We had to wait an extra six months before we could proceed. Now we were together for several years before getting married but was only married a little over three years. And what's really strange to me is I was thinking about getting a divorce a year or so before that happen. I just wasn't feeling happy or appreciated. But I called myself sticking it out for my children. Then that happened but I believe that everything happens for a reason.

And once I was established in my new apartment. I started calling and asking Tamil about getting our children for the weekend. And she would just blow me off. And after me persistently asking for several weeks. I'm told 'once you start paying child support then you'll be able to see and get the children.' That went on for several months. Then suddenly she decided that I could get our children. So, I drove to Detroit to pick up all three of my children. My two children with her and my oldest son.

After getting back to my apartment I noticed that my children with Tamil didn't have a overnight bag with clothes. So, I called Tamil and I told her you didn't send our children with any change of clothes. And I was told 'if you want them to have a change of clothes. Then you need to go and buy them some.' And I told her 'but they both have clothes in their closets with the tags still on them.' 'Again, Sergio if you want them to have a change of clothes then go buy them.' So, out of frustration I just hung up the telephone. I couldn't believe that she was doing this, so I told my children let's go,' as I got them into my car. And I drove to several clothing stores, and I stopped at a furniture store. Where I bought a small four draw dresser for their clothes. And on the way back home. I stopped at a beauty supply store and I bought some things for my daughter's hair.

Chapter 63 'Daddy's Not Coming Back'

I'm getting my children every other weekend now. I always would get them together because I wanted them to grow up being close. After picking up my children and returning to my apartment. I sat my two youngest children down because I wanted to try to explain to them. What happened between me and their mother. And after trying to explain I asked, 'do you guys understand?' And they both said that they do.

I've always spoken to my children as adults. I wanted to have a better relationship with my children then I had with my parents. The one thing about becoming a parent that I felt that my parents taught me. Was to be the total opposite with my children as they were with me. Now I know to some that may seem mean and I understand that but it's true. Although I'm guilty of making some of the same mistakes that my parents made. But for the most part I believe that I've done fairly well, as a father. There're a lot of things that I wish I would've done differently and I hope that my children one day will forgive me. But I know I did the best that I could at that time.

Now I played sports a lot throughout school and I never had a parent or even family at any of my games. So, I know what it feels like not to have that family support for encouragement. That's why I've always tried to make it my business to make it to most of my children's games or events as possible. I made it to most of my son's football games. But I only made it to a few of my daughter's basketball games or recitals. And it wasn't because I didn't want to go at that time. I just didn't have the gas money to drive round trip from my apartment in Westland to her school in Belleville, Michigan. And whenever I would get home from work. I would start thinking about what I told my children and I would start crying. Because I felt they thought I had lied to them about working things out with their mother.

My daughter would call often asking when am I coming back home? And I didn't want to lie, so I just told her the truth 'Daddy's not coming back,' and she would start crying. And once off the telephone with her I would cry like a baby. And with me knowing what I had told her in the basement. But she would consistently call me pleading with me to come back home. And after getting off of the telephone with her. I already felt bad so I would just cry even more.

Then one night on my way home from doing a double shift at Chrysler. There was an accident already on the freeway. And I could see State Troopers and Tow Trucks everywhere. And there were flairs everywhere on the ground, so all of the cars had to merge into one lane. And I had merged already and was at a complete stand still.

Chapter 64 Urgent Care

Then all of a sudden, a car slammed into the back of me, as my head hit the windshield. And the force was so strong that I literally flue back into my seat that's now on top of my back seat. And while struggling to sit myself up a State Police Officer came up to my car and asked, 'are you alright?' And I responded, 'I'll be okay.' Then he said, 'I seen your accident the car that hit you had to be doing 70 mph or more.' I attempted to get out of my car and was told by the State Police Officer 'get back into your car sir and you need to let the ambulance check you out.' I responded, 'no I'll be okay.'

And once back in my car I tried to start my car, but it wouldn't turn over. Then I looked up and I saw the guy that hit me on a stretcher getting into the ambulance. So, I called a friend from work that worked a double with me. And when Jarrell answered I told him that I had a car accident and my car wouldn't start and I asked, 'could you pick me up'? 'Sure, where you at?' 'I'm on I 96 near the Southfield exit.'

After about twenty minutes he arrived. Once inside of his car I called my soon to be x wife and when she answered. I explained what happened and I asked, 'if I could get dropped off over there because it's a lot closer.' She said that I could, and I thanked her, as Jarrell dropped me off at my old house. Once inside I thanked Tamil as I'm sitting on the couch talking to Tamil. And I'm assuming that my daughter heard my voice because she ran out of her bedroom and jumped into my lap. While she's hugging and kissing on me, I said, 'it's really late baby girl you have school in the morning, so you need to go back to bed.' After a few minutes she reluctantly went back into her bedroom.

The following morning, I called a friend for a ride home. Once home I called a rental car company and I had a car delivered. And after dropping off the agent. I was having severe back pain, so I drove myself to the only Urgent Care that I knew off. The DMC Urgent Care Center on 8 mile Road near Lasher.

Once inside I filled out some paperwork and sat and waited. When my name was called, I went back to see the doctor and he said, 'good morning, so what brings you in today?' 'I was in a car accident last night and my back is really sore.' 'Follow me,' as I walked down the hall into another room. Once in the room I'm told 'I want to get some X-rays of your back,' so I moved closer to the X-ray machine. After taking some X-rays I'm told 'you can go back into that other room and once I'm finished with the X-rays. I'll be back in there,' as I returned to the other room.

After about ten minutes the doctor returned and asked, 'have you ever been in war Mr. McGee?' 'No, I haven't so why do you ask?' 'Well looking at your X-rays I seen several white dots,' as I interrupted him and said, 'I've been shot several times many years ago.' 'Okay that explains the dots as bullet fragments,' as he held up an X-ray for me to see. Then he wrote me two prescriptions. One for a muscle stimulator and another for physical therapy.

And after leaving Urgent Care I went straight to the address for physical therapy. Once inside I handed my prescriptions to a woman behind the desk and she said, 'follow me,' as we walked into a large therapy room. Then I'm told 'have a seat and I'll be right back,' as she leaves.

Chapter 65 'What The Hell Is So Funny?'

Once she returned and I'm handed a small package, and she said, 'here's your muscle stimulator and I'll explain how to use that once we're done with your physical therapy.' I performed a multitude of exercises to help with my back. Then I was shown how to use the muscle stimulator. I repeated physical therapy for several weeks and once home.

I opened up my package and there was a small battery-operated machine. With six cords that plugged into the machine and it also had six sticky patches that connected to the cords. I was told to put the patches onto the cord and the cords into the machine. Then I would place the patches onto my back and press the power button. I had to do that three times a day for fifteen minutes at a time. While going to physical therapy I also had to attend court about my divorce.

Once inside of the waiting area outside of the courtroom. Where I saw Tamil and her mother that was seated across the room from me. I'm wondering why is her mother here. They never spoke which I expected so I didn't either. Then after waiting for a while I'm called into the courtroom. Once inside I'm told we have to go before a referee judge first. So, I walked into his office and took a seat beside my lawyer. The referee told Tamil's lawyer to provide, as she started telling the judge a bunch of lies. Saying things like how I don't spend any time with my children. And how I don't help them with their homework and much more. I leaned over to my lawyer and said, 'this is some bullshit nothing she's said is true.' And I'm told 'you'll get your turn to speak Mr. McGee.' And her lawyer continued lying and I couldn't take it anymore more so I interrupted. And the judge said, 'you don't get to speak until you're spoken to,' as the judge told her lawyer to proceed. I only got to answer two questions from the judge. He asked, 'what's your full name and birthdate. Then I asked my lawyer 'when do I get to speak the truth?' 'Not now Mr. McGee, but you'll get your chance soon.' I'm told to come back next week, the same place and time.

The following week I'm in the courtroom again thinking that I'll get to speak this time. The referee judge told Tamil's lawyer to provide again. And her lawyer continued to lie on me even more. Then when I did get to speak it was only to answers the judge questions. He said, 'looking at your paperwork you live in an apartment?' 'Yes, I do.' Then he asks, 'do you have a two bedroom apartment?' I didn't know at that time you had to have two bedrooms with a boy and girl. So, I lied and said, 'yes I do have a two bedroom.' 'That's good' and I didn't get to speak anymore. I was starting to feel the courts are against fathers in a divorce.

Then later that week I had to meet with someone about paying child support. Once I walked into the office, I saw several desks scattered throughout the office. I wasn't sure of where to go, so I asked someone 'where is this person,' as I showed them the name on my envelope. And I was pointed in the right direction and I started walking towards his desk. Once at the desk I introduced myself and we shook hands and I sat across from his desk. Then he asked, 'where do you work at?' 'Chrysler' 'did you bring check stubs like I asked in your letter?' 'Yes, I did,' as I handed them to him. He looked at my stubs and said, 'you'll be paying about 250 a week' and started laughing. So, I asked with an attitude 'what the hell so funny?' 'And how am I supposed to live with so much money being tacking out of my check?' He didn't say anything and just continued to laugh. So, I stood up and slammed my hand on his desk. And when I looked behind me, I saw a Sheriff walking toward me, so I quickly sat back down. And he said, 'I don't care about how you live as long as you pay your child support.' And I said, 'you know that's some bullshit. I'm already paying money for my oldest son.' 'Oh well, that's the amount,' as he just smirked.

Chapter 66 The Following Weekend

As I stood up to leave I whispered, 'you're really lucky that Sheriff is there or I would be whooping your ass right now.' 'I know that's why he's here,' as I walked out slamming the door.

It was time for me to head back to court again. Now it's the actual judge and he asked her lawyer 'what is your client seeking?' And Tamil's lawyer mentioned a lot of things but what stood out to me was when she said, 'my client wants full custody child support and half of his pension.' I didn't get to speak and I wasn't asked anything, so I just sat there feeling frustrated thinking on how this is some real bullshit, as I leave the courtroom.

Once back home I went into the leasing office and asked about moving into a 2-bedroom apartment now. I was told 'we have one available that's next door to your apartment but it will cost you 1300 dollars.' I reluctantly paid the money just in case the judge asked for proof. I must had gone to court over a dozen times. And Tamil ended up getting custody but it wasn't full custody. I was awarded economic custody. Which meant I got to keep my children overnight for 140 days out of the year. She didn't get half of my pension and I didn't have to pay her court cost. And only because of my children I decided to let Tamil keep the house because I could've demanded for the house to be sold and I would've been entitled to have of the sale profit. I really felt that I had been dragged through hell and back. And although I thought it was finally over but it wasn't. I forgot that I had to wait six extra months until my divorce was complete, because of having younger children.

At that time my sister lived across the street from Tamil. And Tamil's mother owned my sister and my mother's house. I'm working even more hours now so I'm able to pay 275 dollars a week in child support. While going through all of this my cellphone rings. And it's my sister asking me to come over to her house.

Once over to her house I'm told to have a seat, so I sat down. And I asked, 'what's up?' She told me 'I have stage 4 Breast Cancer, as I sat there in disbelief. And said, 'are you serious?' 'Yes, I am.' Then I asked, 'so what do you do now to fight this?' 'I'll be starting chemotherapy tomorrow morning and then some radiation.' Then I asked again 'what kind of cancer again?' 'I told you Breast Cancer, as she pressed down on her shirt to show me the massive lump on her breast. Then told me 'the doctor told me the lump is the size of an orange,' as tears begin falling down my face. And she said, 'don't be crying, Sergio I ain't dead yet. I just wanted to tell you myself before you heard it from someone else.' 'So, who all knows about this?' 'Just you and my mother.' 'But enough about that what's going on with your divorce?'

I filled her in with the latest details. And she said, 'I'm so glad that you're getting a divorce, Sergio. Because you already knew that I really didn't care for her, but you wanted to get married anyway. And I already know why but I just wish that you hadn't. And you already know who I think you should be with.' 'I know you been telling me but I messed that up. She's not even speaking to me and I really can't blame her. And I've tried to call her several times but she never answered my calls. I just wanted to apologize for everything and to ask her opinion on whether or not I should've been getting married. We've always been really good friends and I trust her opinion. I just miss her and being able to speak with her about anything. I still have feelings for her but I did have a child with Tamil while we were dating, so I messed that up. But to be really honest I'm glad that were getting a divorce also. I was thinking about getting a divorce years ago. I just don't like how this has all played out with my children.' 'Things don't always go how we want, Sergio. I mean look at my situation I don't want to have Cancer. I don't even smoke and I'm active but sometimes things just happen. You just have to learn to do the best that you can.' 'You're right I just wish Marie would've answered the telephone once.' 'I still think you'll end up being with my friend again one day,' as I hugged her and kissed her on the cheek and left.

Now it's the weekend that I don't have my children, so I'm looking for something to do. Once home I got online and started looking for something or somewhere to go, but I found myself looking up Stage 4 Breast Cancer. And from what I was reading it wasn't looking good. There's only a 10% chance of survival and I started crying.

A few weeks later our grandmother got rushed to the hospital. Once I was notified, I went to visit my grandmother. When I got there, I'm told that her kidneys have failed and it's not looking too good. I called and spoke with my sister and I told her 'I know that you want to come up and visit her, but with your immune system being weak. I don't think that you should,' so we decided that she wouldn't come to the hospital.

The next day I'm back at the hospital and her doctor thought that I was one of her sons, so I played along thinking I'll get more information. A lot of my family was at the hospital and I decided to go into my grandmother's room. When I entered into the room. I couldn't believe how much she looked like my mother laying there as I started crying.

After about twenty minutes I came out of the room. And my youngest brother Michael had entered into the room. Then shortly after he came out of the room crying while saying 'she looks like our mother laying there,' as we hugged and cried.

A few days later unfortunately I'm told that she had passed away. And most of my family was back at the hospital just like when my grandfather had passed. It's starting to seem that my family only gets together when someone has passed away. The following weekend I went to my grandmother's funeral that was on W. Mc Nicholas and Schaefer.

Chapter 67 We Switched Keys

She wanted to be cremated and there was a viewing for family and friends prior to her being cremated. I'm dealing with death cancer and my divorce. And I'm still recording music but not as much. I was writing a lot because it has always been a way for me to vent my feelings. I've always found writing to be therapeutic.

My sister didn't seem to be getting any better and with her recent hair loss. She decided to cut her hair really short. While talking on the telephone with my auntie her mother. I'm told 'she hasn't been eating much and when she does it's very little.' So, I went over to my sister's house and once inside I walked back into her bedroom. And I asked, 'what's going on why you're not eating?' And I'm told 'I just don't really have an appetite to eat.' So, her mother went out and purchased some Ensure Shakes, so whenever she didn't feel like eating. She could drink a shake and get some kind of nutrition.

I started spending a lot of my time over my sister's house. I became really concerned about her not eating and everything else. And she would always call me whenever my soon to be x wife would have her new friend over at the house. And whenever I would come to visit with my sister. I would always sit on the couch that was in front of the living room window. Where I could peek through the blinds If I chose and see Tamil's house.

One time while visiting my sister she said, 'I'll be right back, Sergio I need to make a run.' And I told her 'my truck is in front of yours in the driveway, so just take my truck but leave me your keys in case I need to leave before you get back.' 'Okay,' as we switched keys. While sitting on the couch. I heard a vehicle in front of the house so I peeked through the blinds and I saw a van in the middle of the street. Then I seen Tamil get out of the van and walked into the house. Now I know this guy drives a van so I wrote down the license plate. Then I called a friend that worked at the Secretary of State. Once I gave her the plate number, she gave me the name and address of the person the vehicle was registered to.

Once my sister got back home and we talked for a while. Then I left to go home and once home. I started doing what I called my "home work "on her friend. Where I would gather as much information as possible about a certain person. And after a few hours I had all the information that I needed to know. I did that because I wanted to know what he may be capable of doing if it ever became a physical street beef.

It was my weekend to get my children. But I was only able to pick up my oldest son because Tamil wouldn't let me get our two children. After picking up my oldest son on Friday. It was on Saturday evening when I called Tamil on her cellphone. I was calling about getting the rest of my things out of her basement. Once she answered she got real nasty with me for whatever reason and hung up the telephone. So, I called back and she hung up again, so now I'm feeling that something isn't right. I told my son to get into my vehicle and we drove to her house in Detroit. Now for those that may not be familiar. That's a good twenty minute drive but I got there in about ten minutes. I parked down the street from her house and just waited.

Then after a few minutes I saw that van pull up and Tamil got out with what looked like a overnight bag. I didn't care about that but it explained why she was getting nasty with me, so I waited a few more minutes. Until she was into the house and I called and she said, 'this isn't good time, Sergio I'm in bed.' 'I just want to get the rest of my stuff out of the basement. It will take me maybe five minutes Tamil.' 'This isn't a good time I was asleep' as I pulled into the driveway. And said, 'I'm in your driveway now.' 'I told you this wasn't a good time, Sergio,' as she hung-up the telephone. While sitting in the driveway I saw her mother pull up in front of the house. Then I looked and I seen a guy in her car, as she walked by my vehicle. Then she started knocking on the side door and when Tamil answered they started talking. Then Tamil yelled at me 'what do you want, Sergio?' I rolled down my window and I said, 'I already told you I just want to get the rest of my stuff that's in the basement. I could've used my key but I called.' 'I've changed the locks, Sergio so you wouldn't been able to enter the house.' 'That's fine I called you first anyway and why did you call your mother'? 'I didn't know what you might do so I called my mother'? 'Wow really Tamil you didn't need to call your mother' as I got out and stood next to my vehicle. And said, 'you know what I'll just get my stuff some other time' as I got back into my vehicle. And while driving back home I'm wondering why Tamil felt it was necessary to call her mother. I've never put my hands on her so why?

Once at home I looked into my back seat and my son was asleep. So, I picked him up and I carried him into my apartment. Once inside I placed him into a bed and removed his coat and shoes.

Then later that month I went over to my uncle Damon's house to watch the Tyson fight. And just as the fight had ended my cellphone rings and it's my sister telling me that 'Tamil's friend is over to the house again.

Chapter 68 'I Won't Blame You'

I jumped into my truck and drove over to my sister's house. With my music blasting "I ant no joke." When I got out of my truck and I'm assuming that she heard my music because she came to the door. I looked across the street and saw the guy's van in Tamil's driveway, so I called Tamil's cellphone. And when she answered I asked 'why do you have him in there with my children home?. If y'all wanted to fuck that bad go get a damn room.' Then we started arguing and she hung up the telephone. I called back and she hung up again, so I started yelling towards the house. Asking the guy to come outside so we can talk about this' as I stood there holding my handgun. Then I yelled 'if you want to fight then we can fight. And I'll plant your ass in this yard unless you're scared of me you punk bitch!'

Then Tamil's little sister KeKe pulled up and as she was going into the house. I asked, 'if my children are in the house let me know please?' 'Okay' and after a few minutes. She came to the door and said, 'they're in the house' and now I'm really pissed. So, I started yelling even louder saying 'why can't y'all go to a motel instead of fucking in there with my children!' And my sister came onto the porch and started calling my name saying, 'Sergio come over here,' as I slowly walked over near her porch. And she said, 'you're high and pissed if she called the police your ass is going to jail.' 'No, I'm not that's my house to my license still have that address,' as I pointed towards the house. And she said, 'you have a gun and you don't think you're going to jail okay I told you.' 'I'm sorry you're right, but my children are in there.' 'I know and she's trifling for that but you don't need to go to jail now. That's not going to help you in your divorce.' 'You're right I'm leaving,' as I kissed her on the cheek. And she said, 'call me when you get home, Sergio.' 'I will and I'm sorry again,' as I got into my truck.

Once home I called her and she asked, 'have you calmed down yet, Sergio?' 'Hell no why would she have him there with my children.' 'I know I told you, Sergio it was just something about her that I didn't like.'

The weekend after I acted a fool over Tamil's house. I went to pick up all of my children. And once I got my children inside of my apartment. I sat them down and started apologizing for everything that they've dealt with cause of my divorce. 'I know this hasn't been easy for you two,' as I pointed to Denzel and Nichole. 'I lost my temper last week and you guys should've never heard that so that will never happen again and I'm sorry. And now that I've apologized let's do something fun, but it has to be something that your sister wants to do also.' I'm given a few things that we could do but there'll all things for boys. Then I suggested going to an arcade. That way there will be things to do for everyone. They became excited about that idea. So, we got into my truck and drove to Marvin's Marvelous Mechanical Museum.

Once inside I purchased forty dollars' worth of tokens. And after several hours and after getting them more tokens and something to eat there. I easily spent well over hundred dollars, but it was well worth it because I got to spend some quality time with my children.

Then on Sunday morning I told them to place their packed bags near my front door. And when we were about to leave my daughter asked, 'why can't I stay here with you daddy?' 'Baby girl you got to go to school, so I'm thinking I've answered her question. Then she looked up at me and said, 'I can go to school out here daddy.' 'But you're already in a really good school and I don't want to take you out.'

Then as we walked out of the door and once in my truck. As I'm about to start up my truck I looked into my rearview mirror. And I seen all of them watching to see if I would put on my seatbelt before pulling off. I had made a wager with my children that we all would wear our seatbelts whenever in a car. And if I didn't, I would have to pay each of them fifty cents but if they didn't, I would be owed twenty five cents. So, when I put on my seatbelt and started up the truck. "All man" is all I heard from the back seat, as I started laughing and drove them home.

Then after about eight months of not dating and going to the movies alone. I wanted to try to catch up with Marie once again. So, I called my sister and I asked her to call Marie and have her call me please? 'I'll give her your number to call you, but if she doesn't call don't blame me.' 'I won't blame you but I really would like to speak with her and if for nothing else to apologize.' Then she reminded me on how I messed things up with Marie. 'I already know that you don't have to keep reminding me okay. I just want to talk with her okay.' 'What's in it for me?' 'What you mean?' 'What do I get?' 'My appreciation isn't good enough, so what do you want?' 'I'm not sure but I'll let you know.

Chapter 69 I Filled Out The Application

Then later that day I got a telephone call from Marie. And I'm nervously excited as we begin to talk. And after I apologizing several times. We just started talking as if we had never stopped speaking. After a few telephone calls I decided to ask her out on a date if you will and she agreed and I believe we went to the movies.

Now even when I was married, I would always keep tabs on Marie unbeknown to her. I just wanted to make sure that she was okay. And whenever she would have a problem. I would do a few things behind the scenes to "fix" the problem. With me being street related if you will. I was able to find out and do certain things that others may not be able to do that's legal or illegal. I always went out with Marie on the opposite weekends that I would have my children. And after a year or so we started dating again and I was very happy about that. Because I had been so mad and sad for so long. While dealing with death, divorce and cancer.

After over a year of dating Marie I decided to introduce her to my children. I was very apprehensive about that at first because I had my daughter while I was dating Marie. But once they meet, I was presently surprised on how well Marie seemed to be with my children. And they also seemed to like her as well.

I was very happy that she already knew how to cook and she would come over to my apartment sometimes to visit. And she would cook and clean and I would just sit there watching and be thinking to myself. On how I'm such a fool for not trying to marry her.

Then shortly after I moved into a bigger apartment but I'm still in Westland, Michigan. The new apartment had a swimming pool and it's near Hines Park. I knew that my children would love having a pool. And I already knew that my credit had taken a beaten during my divorce, but I wanted a DVD player that I seen in an ABC Warehouse sales paper. And there was an ABC Warehouse around the corner from my apartment. So I decided to go and once inside of the store a salesman approach me. And he asked if I would like to fill out a credit application. And I would receive a 10% discount on my purchase. I said, 'sure' as I filled out the application. Then I started looking for the DVD player. After about ten minutes the salesman found me and said, 'you've been approved.' 'Are you sure?' 'Yes, you've been approved.' So, I'm thinking for 250 dollars, so I asked, 'for how much?' '5,500 dollars.' 'Are you serious?' 'I am,' so I put down the DVD player and started shopping. I ended up getting myself a 52 inch floor model television. A Kenwood surround sound with 5 disc CD changer and speakers with stands. Then once at the register I handed the young lady behind the register my application. And she ringed me up and told me 'everything that you've purchased will be delivered to your residence tomorrow.'

Once I got back to my apartment. I put my 19 inch television into my bedroom and the following weekend. I had picked up my children and I never told them about what I had gotten. And when we walked into my apartment and my children looked and saw the big-screen television near the door and they gasps. I can't lie that felt good because I told myself after my divorce. That I wanted to live, as good or better as if I was still married.

The following weekend Marie came over and we went to a furniture store. And once inside of the store and just like at the warehouse. A salesman approached me to fill out a credit application. So, I filled out the application and we started looking around. The salesman came up to me and told me that 'you've been approved for 2,200 dollars' and I couldn't believe that I had been approved. So, I started looking at living room sets. And Marie had suggested something that she liked, so I went to go look.

Chapter 70 'Next Weekend'

At a big tan couch/sectional that I thought was beautiful, so I ended up purchasing. The next day without Marie I went to Target to look for a coffee and end tables. I found and bought some all-black wooden tables. Once home I assembled the tables and rearrange my furniture.

Now finally my place was looking how I wanted, and everything seemed to be going really well. I have a new apartment a crossover SUV and furniture with credit cards. Then I got a telephone call and my auntie Beth told me about my sister having seizures. So, I decided to go over to her house.

Once inside I'm told she's in the bed so I walked back into her bedroom. And when I opened up her bedroom door and seen that she was asleep. So, I closed her door and walked back into the living room and sat on the couch. And my auntie started telling me 'she's never done that before and that freaked me out. And I didn't know what to do so I called you, Sergio I'm sorry.' I told her 'there's no need to apologize. I want you to call me about anything dealing with her but you need to notify her doctor about this.' 'I'll be calling him in the morning.' And after a few hours I decided to leave and while driving home. I'm thinking about everything that she told me and tears started falling.

Once home it was late, so I took a shower. And I'm still thinking about my sister and before getting into bed. I got on my knees and started praying like I've always done. And after my prayers I asked an extra prayer for my sister. That she lives and gets better. Then I got into the bed but I couldn't sleep. I was still thinking about my sister and after a few hours I fell asleep.

The next morning, I had to work and after getting dressed. I went to work and while at work I decided to look in on getting my FMLA papers. Once I found out that I didn't have them yet, so I got with my Union Rep. and got my papers straighten out. I was thinking I may need them soon, but I'm hoping that I won't.

After work and once home, I called my sister and her mother answered the telephone. And I asked, 'how is she doing?' 'She's doing okay.' 'Can I talk to here?' 'Sure, hold on,' as she got onto the telephone. And I asked, 'how are you feeling?' 'I'm good but I don't want to talk about me being sick okay?' 'That's fine.' Then she asked, 'how are your children doing?' 'They're getting bigger.' 'I know I saw Nicole riding her bike yesterday and she's gotten a lot bigger. And she looks like you just spit her out. Y'all even have that same damn frown.' 'Yeah I know, as I started laughing while saying 'she's a daddy girl.' Then she said, 'also, Sergio I have something to give you.' And I asked, 'what is it?' 'Don't worry I'll give it to you but not right now.' 'Why can't I know what it is?' 'I hate that I even said something now because you don't need to know right now.' 'Okay that's fine, so what are you doing today?' 'I'm thinking about watching my team play softball today.' 'That's cool I know you miss playing don't you,' as she explained her love for playing baseball. I asked, 'do you want me to go with you today?' 'No not this one I know you have to work, but there's a game next Sunday at Softball City, so you could come with me to that game.'

That following Sunday we went to the game. While sitting on the bleachers as I'm watching her coach Third Base. I could see how much she missed playing. And I felt at least she's a part of the game that I know she loves by helping to coach. I knew for those few hours of the game she's not thinking about being sick. And that made me happy because I knew she was happy.

Now I had been asking my sister for months to spend the night over my apartment. And whenever she wouldn't come over, I would just come over and spend the night at her house. And when she finally said, 'yes I'll come over so you'll stop begging.' I was so excited and I asked, 'so when?' 'Next weekend.' 'Okay, but you know that's Valentine's Day weekend right?' 'I know it's not like I have a date, so is that a bad time for you? Because if so, I don't have to come.' 'No, it's not a bad time for me I just didn't know if you realized.

150

Chapter 71 'This Is What I Wanted To Give You'

'I'm just glad that you finally agreed to come over.' And when I got to work on Monday. I told them that I won't be able to work on Friday or the weekend. Once off work I went straight home and straighten up my place.

Then on Friday afternoon Valentine's day I drove over to pick up my sister. Once inside as she came out of her bedroom while holding a bad. I grabbed the bag as we walked to my truck. After helping her into my truck I put her bag into my back seat and started driving. While driving I'm asked, 'why are you smiling so much?' 'Because you're finally coming over after months of me asking you.' Once at my apartment I helped her out of my truck. Then I grabbed her bag and we walked into my apartment.

Once inside she started looking around and I asked, 'what's wrong?' 'I'm just checking my surrounding' and I started laughing. And said, 'really? you're more than safe over here trust me.' I took her coat and bag and I placed them onto my bed. And when I returned I asked, 'so what do you want to do first? A movie or video game?' As I sat next to her on my couch. And surprisingly we played the PlayStation first and then we watched a movie.

Then after the movie she asked for some water to take her medication. So I went into the kitchen and got her a glass of water. Then after taken her medication she wanted to lay down, so I showed her to my bedroom. And I told her 'just lay her' and I went back into the living room. And she slept a lot while at my place, so I just sleep on my couch.

Once Sunday came around. And after taking her medication she got back into my bed. Then she asked me for something to drink, so I went and got her some water. When I entered my bedroom to give her the water. She asked, 'lay on the bed with me,' so I got onto the bed. And we started reminiscing about what we've been through together. And I asked her 'what is this all about?' As she reached onto the side of the bed and pulled an envelope out of her bag. And said, 'this is what I wanted to give to you,' as she handed me the envelope. And said, 'but you can't open that envelope until I pass, Sergio.' 'Don't say that' 'you know what I mean.' 'So, why me and not your mother'? 'Because I know she'll still be in grief. And she won't be in any kind of condition to do anything, but I know that you will.' 'That's true,' as I started crying. And she said stop crying, Sergio,' as she wiped my tears. And I said, 'you know the last time you wiped my tears I was in the hospital and I couldn't speak. Then I asked, 'do you remember that?' 'How could I forget.' 'You were the only one that understood what I was trying to say, 'I remember that,' as we both started laughing. We laid in my bed for hours reminiscing on the good and bad times that we've shared. Then I said, 'I need to get you home,' so I got off the bed. And went into my living room, as she yelled 'don't show anyone what's in that envelope, Sergio.' 'I'm not, now here's your coat,' as I handed her, her coat.

Once in my truck as I'm driving, she said, 'I'm serious, Sergio don't show anyone.' 'I've told you that I'm wouldn't,' so stop telling me that okay.' I knew that she was on a chicken nugget kick, so I stopped at a Micky Dee's. And I ordered her some nuggets and fries, because I new if she didn't eat them now, she would later.

Once I got her into the house, I stayed for about an hour and then I left. Once home I took a quick shower shave and changed my clothes. Then I drove to Allen Park, Michigan to pick up Marie. I wanted to take her to both a movie and dinner but we missed the starting time for the movie, so we just went to a restaurant.

About three months after my sister spent the weekend at my place. I got a telephone call telling me that she had been rushed to the hospital. I was at work when I got the call, so I decided to finish my shift. And the whole time that I'm working I'm worried about my sister. After about two hours it's finally time for me to get off. And once in my truck while driving I called my auntie and asked, 'are you still at the hospital'? 'Yes, I am.' 'What hospital? 'Okay I'm on my way right now, so do you need me to bring you anything up there'? 'No, I mean yeah some cigarettes and a pop please.' 'Okay I'll stop and grabbed that before coming up there.' 'Okay please hurry, Sergio.' 'I'm on my way now,' as I got off of the telephone..

Chapter 72 "I Will'

I'm really worried that she said to hurry. So, I'm thinking it must be really bad. I stopped at a store and grabbed a pop and some cigarettes. Then once I arrived at the parking garage at the hospital. I got out of my truck and called my auntie as I started walking towards the hospital. And asked, 'where are you at in the hospital?' 'Okay I'm right outside,' as I walked into the hospital.

It took me several minutes before I approached my auntie that's sitting on a wooden bench in the hallway. I could tell that she had been crying. As I walked up and handed her a bag and she said, 'thank you.' Then I asked, 'where is my sister?' She pointed across the hall, as she sipped her pop. Then she said, 'I had to step out of there, Sergio I didn't want her to see me crying.' And I said, 'I'm going to go see her' 'go ahead but she's asleep,' so I walked towards the room not knowing what to expect. I'm really nervous as I entered into the room.

She appeared to be asleep, so I looked at her chest to see if she's breathing and she was, so I turned to walk out of the room. When I heard her whisper 'Sergio,' so I turned around and said, 'I thought you were asleep. And I didn't want to wake you,' as I walked towards her bed. And she said, 'yeah right you were looking to see if I was breathing right?' I started to lie, then she interrupted and said, 'don't lie, Sergio I know you,' as I started laughing. And said, 'yeah you're right' 'I knew it,' as we both started laughing. I sat in a chair near her bed and she asked, 'so how's my mom doing?' 'She's doing as good as one could expect considering.' 'I'm worried about her, Sergio.' 'She'll be fine we're worried about you right now.' Then she asked, 'you haven't shown that note to anyone?' 'No, I haven't, so stop asking please you said just to do whatever it says whenever that time comes.' 'That's good I was just checking.' 'I don't want you asking me about that anymore please?' 'Okay I'm sorry.' 'No, you're not,' 'but I love you, Sergio,' as she started laughing. 'Since you're up now I'm going to go get your mother okay I'll be right back.' And I walked out of the room and I didn't see her mother anywhere in the hallway. So, I went back into her room and said, 'I don't see your mother anywhere.' 'She's probably somewhere smoking a cigarette.' And I said, 'you're probably right I did bring her some up here.

Then after about ten minutes she walked into the room complaining. About having to walk out into the parking lot to smoke. 'That's why you need to quit smoking period mom. My auntie would usually have a quick clap back but this time she just agreed. I was waiting in my sister's room for her doctor to arrive saying that everything is fine and that she could go home now. After several hours he finally came into the room. He asked me to step out and she said, 'that's my brother,' as he looked shocked. Then my auntie said, 'that's her brother.' 'Okay I'm afraid we're going to have to keep you here a little longer. I need to get some more blood work done and I want to run a few tests also' and he leaves the room. And I said, 'we might as well get comfortable,' as I grabbed a pillow. 'What do you mean we?' 'I'm staying, and I'll leave when you leave you do remember telling me that when I was in the hospital right?' 'Do you know how long ago that was, Sergio?' 'Yes, I do, it was in April of 1990. 'You don't have to stay up here, Sergio.' 'I'll leave when you leave.' 'You heard what the doctor said right?' 'I did' as I adjusted the pillow. 'That chair isn't like your bed, Sergio. 'I know but it will do.'

And after about three hours we both were asleep. And my auntie woke me up and I got up and said, 'here take my chair because I already know that you're staying.' 'Thank you for coming, Sergio.' 'No need to be thanking me that's my sister over there. There's no way I wouldn't be up her,' as I walk towards the door. And she asked me 'call me when you get home, Sergio.' 'I will' as I walked out of the door.

Chapter 73 That Maybe True, Sergio

While driving home I'm praying that my sister doesn't die. Once home I called my auntie. Then said my prayers and got into my bed.

The next day once dressed I drove back up to the hospital. And once I got into the hospital, I saw my auntie in the hallway. And she started telling me how my sister's condition had gotten worse. I'm told her doctors came in and told them that her cancer has spread to her brain.' And I asked does my sister know?' 'Yes, she does he said that to both of us while in her room.' Then I asked, 'so what is her doctor talking about doing now?' 'He's saying there's nothing else that they can do and there talking about putting her into hospice.' 'What's that?' 'Were they'll place her on another floor in the hospital and try to keep her as comfortable as possible until she dies.' 'What,' as I got physical upset and loudly said, 'that's some bullshit'! 'Boy watch your mouth.' And I said, 'with all this fucking technology in this hospital. They weren't saying that shit yesterday.' 'They were able to tell from the blood test, Sergio.' They're supposed to move her to a different floor and room soon. 'I just don't understand how you go from blood work to hospice in a day.' 'I agree, but there's nothing else that we can do.' 'With all this fucking equipment and technology this is some real bullshit,' as I stormed off. And walked around until I found a hospital chapel.

Once I found a chapel I looked inside and I didn't see anyone in there, so I went in and sat up in the front. I started praying and I'm asking God why my sister? She doesn't deserve this, as I gathered myself then walked back.

Once back with my auntie I'm told that 'she's been moved to hospice, Sergio.' I'm assuming that she called our family because there were some family members up there visiting. My family didn't know about her being sick until I believe until the day before. So, I'm trying to let them visit with her, so I stayed away. I know that may seem selfish of me, but I didn't care. I just wanted to spend as much time as possible alone with my sister and after several hours of waiting. I went into her room and when I entered the room. I seen two of my aunties and an uncle. There wasn't anywhere for me to seat, so I stood in the corner. I'm staring at her as everyone was talking and I'm thinking about her dying and my eyes became tearing. So, I walked out of the room and into the nearest restroom.

Once in there I began crying profusely. Once done I wiped my face and walked back into her room. And some family was still in there, so I told her 'I'll be back. I'm going to get myself something to eat, so do you want anything?' 'Nope I'm good,' so I leave the room. As I'm walking through the hospital, I saw an ATM machine. And after getting myself some money out I walked out of the hospital and into the parking garage.

Once in my truck I drove to the McDonalds that was nearest to the hospital. I got myself a combo meal and some chicken nuggets for my sister. Once back at the hospital and into her room. I seen that one of my aunties had left but there's more family up there. So, I decided to go out into the hallway. And I sat on the bench to eat and once done eating. I went back into her room and I placed the bag with the nuggets on her table. After she looked and saw the bag then said, 'I was going to ask you to get me some nuggets,' as she grabbed the bag. 'I know they're in the bag.' 'You think you know me don't you, Sergio?' 'There in the bad, so yeah I do,' as I walked out of the room.

After a while I came back into the room and sat next to her bed and she told me 'you know I've seen more family today. Then I've seen all year Sergio. "Yeah, I know you're real popular now, but to be fair they just found out that you're sick.' 'That maybe true, Sergio, but it shouldn't be that way.' 'I agree, but that's how are family is right now. So, I'm about to leave now, so you can get some rest and I'll be back in the morning.' 'Okay but I'll be bored' 'but why? you should be resting, so why do you say that?' 'There's nothing to watch on this television. I need some cable or a DVD player with some real movies.' 'So, what are you trying to say?' 'I want to see things like "Raw" with Eddie Murphy or "The Golden Child" you know movie like that.' 'I'll see what I can do but just try to get some rest tonight please. 'Okay I'll try." And I'll see you tomorrow. I love you and try to be nicer to your mother please.' 'I am being nice to her, so get out of here boy,' as I walked out of the door.

Chapter 74 'I'm Sick Of Being Sick'

Once home I took a shower and said my prayers and got into my bed. But I couldn't sleep, so I just laid there until I fell asleep.

The following morning, I got dressed and went to the hospital. I got there around 10:30 am. And I saw my auntie and I told her 'you really need to go home you've already been up here for a few days now. You need to take a shower and get some real rest. I know you would like to lay in your own bed, right?' She didn't say anything so I continued. 'I'm up her now, so you can just go home please'. And she said, 'no I'm good Sergio.' 'No, you're not good and If you keep this up, you'll be right in here with her, so you should go now. While all of these people are up here visiting. And if anything, happens, I'll just call and you can come back up here, so please just go she'll be fine I'm up here.' 'I'll go home, Sergio but I'll be back in a few hours.' 'That's fine just go home please,' as she leaves. And while walking away she said, 'you better call me if something happens you hear me, Sergio?' 'Yeah now go home please.' I didn't bother to tell my sister that her mother went home. And if she was to ask, I would just tell her that she must have went outside for a cigarette.

Then later that afternoon my auntie returned, and I asked, 'don't you feel a lot better now?' 'Yes, I do, you were right, Sergio, so how is she doing?' 'She's good some friends are in there with her now. And other people have been coming up to see here all day including family. I don't even think she knows that you were gone.' 'So, who's in there with her now?' ''I believe your sister and brother,' as we both went into her room. Once in the room I asked my sister 'do you need anything?' 'I could use some ice water,' so I went to go get her some ice water. When I got back and I gave her the water. And said, 'I'll be back, I have to make a run,' as I left the room.

Once home I grabbed my PlayStation and a few video games. Then I went to a video store and I rented the movies that she mentioned. Then I headed back up to the hospital. Once I got into her room, I'm asked, 'where have you been?' 'I told you I needed to make some runs, so why are you asking me that?' 'Because you come in here with your black backpack and I just want to know.' 'You're just nosy, but anyway I went and got my PlayStation, and a few games and I also rented the movies that you wanted to see. Now I just need to hook this up to your television,' as I began connecting everything.

And after about twenty minutes I was done. And I said, 'you owe me big for this,' as we started laughing. Then I asked, 'so what do you want to do first, a movie or a video game?' 'I need to laugh, so put on Raw,' as I put the DVD into my PlayStation. And we're both cracking up, as were watching that movie. I had forgot how funny that movie was. And when the movie went off, we just started talking. And she told me since she's been sick, she's never felt scared, but how she finds herself being scared now. And I told her 'you just have to keep praying and fighting. That's what I had to do when I was shot. We don't know the outcome, so our faith has to be its strongest.' 'Look at you, talking to me about faith you know that's crazy right? I mean from the outside to a lot of people. You're this big bag drug dealing rapper, but people don't know this side of you, you need to let people see this side of you more.' 'I'm getting there it's just gonna take me some time.' 'I don't have a lot of time left, Sergio.' 'What do you mean?' And she started telling me how her cancer had spread to her brain. 'Just remember the doctor doesn't have the final say so, only God dose.' 'I know that, Sergio, but it's not looking good. I'm just getting tired of being sick.' 'I know we're all tired of you being sick also but you can't give up fighting.' 'I'm not but I'm just tired.' 'I know,' as I rubbed her leg. 'I'm about to go, so please get some rest tonight and I'll be back in the morning. I love you,' as I walked out of the door.

Once in my truck, as I'm driving home. I'm thinking about what she said. "I'm just tired of being sick." That was the first time that I ever heard her complain about being sick, so for her to say that now had me really scared.

Chapter 75 'Are You Sure'

Once home surprisedly I got about six hours of sleep. The following morning, I went back up to the hospital. And once into her room we started talking. Then she started speaking about our cousin Tina, that lives in Atlanta, Georgia. And about twenty minutes later Tina walked into the room. I was shocked as I stood up to huge Tina and I told her 'we were just talking about you.' Then she walked over to my sister's bed and bent over to hug and kiss her, as I grabbed her a chair.

Then we all started talking about everything but cancer. And we stayed up there at the hospital with my sister for a few days without leaving. And we watched every movie several times and played the video game some, but mostly we just talked. And that was something that we hadn't done since we were preteens. And after not changing my clothes or showering. I was smelling pretty bad. So, I told them 'I'm going home to shower and change my clothes. And I'll be back up later today or tomorrow morning' and I left out of the room. Once I got home, I took a shower and fell asleep.

The next morning after getting dressed. I drove back up to the hospital. And once inside of my sister's room. I noticed that Tina was gone, so I just assumed that she went to take a shower and change her clothes as well. After visiting with my sister for a few hours I leave.

The next day I returned to the hospital and I saw my auntie Beth and she started telling me about what happened last night. 'She seen Jesus in the corner of her room.' 'Are you serious?' 'Yes, I am she keep asking me do I see him?' 'See who?' No, I don't. Then she keep saying how she's not ready to go yet,' and she kept pointed at the corner. 'So, did you tell her doctor about this?' 'I did already and he's saying with the cancer spreading to her brain that could be the reason for that. 'I'm telling you, Sergio she saw something in that corner. She kept pointing and talking to something like I'm talking to you right now.' I found that to be weird because I was just up there the other night. And we were talking and laughing and now this! Then I asked, 'how is she doing now?' 'She's sleeping now.' 'I'm about to go in there.' 'You can go ahead but she's sleeping,' as I walked into the room.

When I entered, she was asleep, so I sat in the chair next to her bed. And while I was sitting, I started staring at her, as I'm thinking about everything that I've been told. And what she told me about being tired of being sick. With tears running down my face as I placed my hand on her leg and I began to pray. I'm asking God that she doesn't die, but I don't want for her to suffer anymore. I wiped my tears from my face and walked out of the room.

Then I seen my auntie in the hallway, so I gave her a hug and took a seat next to her on the bench. And I asked her 'how are you doing?' 'I'll be okay.' And after a few hours I asked, 'do you need anything?' 'No' 'okay well, I'm about to leave, so if you need anything just call me okay?' 'I will.' 'Promise me that you'll call.' 'I will, Sergio you know you're starting to sound just like you sister with all of that promise me stuff,' as I got up and walked away.

As I'm walking towards my truck my eyes began to get really watery. Once inside of my truck I started crying and on my drive home I was crying. Once home I just cried myself to sleep. My auntie Beth birthday is tomorrow and I would hate for her daughter to pass away on her birthday. I was still going up to the hospital every day but I wasn't staying overnight or as long. It just became to draining and sad. I was still hoping and praying that something would change and change soon. But all of my praying doesn't seem to be working, so I didn't know what else to do. It had been only a week since we were talking and laughing.

Once I got up to the hospital and inside of her room. We started talking about last week when Tina was up there, and we all were watching movies and talking. And a few hours had passed and my uncle Lamar had come to visit my sister. And about an hour later my cousin Simone, and then my auntie Marie came, so I gave my auntie my seat. And after a few hours my uncle said, 'let's go to the casino to get something to eat.' And I said, 'I'm good you guys go ahead.' Then Simone said, 'let's go, Sergio we'll be right back the casino is only ten minutes away. We'll be back before you know it.' Not wanting to go, but I reluctantly went. And my auntie Marie said, 'I'll stay here with her, so if anything happens, I'll just call.' I was having strong feeling that I shouldn't go, but I went anyway.

When we got into the casino and I was right where they checked for your identification. And as I was pulling out my license my uncle's cellphone rings and I heard him say 'okay. Then he said, 'we need to go back up to the hospital now' with tears in his eyes, so I asked, 'what's wrong?' He wouldn't look at me and just said, 'she passed away.' And tears just started falling down my face, as I loudly said, 'I knew I shouldn't have come' and got into his car.

Once back at the hospital. I saw my aunties in the hallway hugging and crying in front of my sister room. I asked my auntie Marie 'what happen?' 'I was just sitting there and I heard her take a deep gasp of breath, so I looked at the machine and it had flat lined, so I ran out of the room to go get the nurse. Once the nurse came back into the room. She pronounced her died and that's when I called your uncle.' 'Is anyone in the room with her now?' 'No' well, I'm going in there,' as I walked into the room.

While crying I slowly pulled a chair up near her bed. Then I grabbed her hand and I started praying. After praying I am apologizing for leaving and I said, 'but knowing you, you would've waited until I left to leave me. I'm just glad that you're in a better place and not suffering anymore.' Then I got up and stood over her bed and kissed her on the forehead. 'I love you and I will miss you,' as I stood there staring and crying. Then I grabbed her hand and said, 'I love you' and walked out of the room.

Once in the hallway I saw my auntie Beth sitting on the bench crying. So, I walked over towards her and she stood up and we hugged and cried. Then I asked, 'so now what?' 'I called the funeral home already so I just have to wait for them to pick her up.' 'Is it OH Pye Funeral home?' 'Yeah that's where she wanted her funeral service.' 'Okay because she told me that also, so you can go home and I'll wait for them to pick her up.' 'Are you sure?' 'Yeah I'm sure just go home and do whatever it is that you need to do and I'll see you at the house after they come get here.'

Once she leaves, I went back into her room and I sat down and started crying. Then I started talking to her, as if she was still alive. 'I guess I can open that envelope now.' After a few hours the guys arrived to get my sister. And I stood there and watched as they placed her body onto a stretcher. And I followed them out of the hospital until they had her placed inside of the truck.

Chapter 76 Magazine Style

Once in my truck I cried, as I drove to my sister's house. When I arrived, I stayed for several hours. And some family members had came over to spend the night. And after a while I decided to leave.

Once home I went straight into my bedroom and grabbed the envelope. When I opened the envelope there were two sheets of paper. I pulled them out and begin to read the first paper. That read 'if you're reading this now that means you've opened this up too early and you're just nosy. But if not, that means I've passed and you waited like I've asked. First, I just want you to know that I love you, Sergio. There are somethings that I want you to do for me please. I have life insurance, so that should cover all of my funeral expenses. My mother knows we're my insurance papers are and here's a list of things that I want to be done", as I began reading several things that she listed. I had promised her that I would do whatever she asked so I will.

I got with my auntie Beth a day or so later to purchase a casket. And after looking at several caskets. We ended up getting one that we both like and it's also similar to what she wrote in the note. Then we went to Green Lawn Cemetery on Grand River near Telegraph to purchase a plot. After being shown several areas of plots. I told the guy that I want an area where I can purchase two side by side plots. 'That's no problem there's a plot for sale right by the plot you already liked. My sister wanted two plots one for her and the other for her mother. After purchasing the plots. Then we went across the street to look at headstones.

After looking around my auntie pick one and purchased it. When she went to pay, I told the salesman that I wanted her picture put on there as I gave him the picture. And this information on there as well as I handed him a piece of paper with the information. And I told him 'I have two plots that are side by side. So, I want her information on one side of the headstone and just leave the other side blank.

Now we had done all of these things within a couple of days. And she wanted her funeral service to be held at the same funeral home as our grandfather. OH Pye Funeral Home. We went to the funeral home and my auntie made the arrangements for her service and viewing. Then my auntie went somewhere to pick her up something to wear for the funeral. And I told her 'she wanted to wear something peach auntie.' 'Yeah, I know she told me also, Sergio.' And she even wrote in the letter what song she wanted played during her service. And it was the same song that played at our grandfather's funeral. "Don't Cry for Me" by Bebe and Cece Winans. After getting everything together for her funeral. We still needed to create a funeral program.

So, myself along with several of my aunties and cousins. Got together over my auntie Beth house with a bunch of pictures of my sister with different members of our family. And there were so many pictures that we couldn't include all of them. It took us several hours to decide on which pictures to include. I became so obsessed with everything because I wanted to make sure that everything was perfect for her home going. But looking back on my behavior now I was just trying to remain busy to keep from dealing with my grief. My auntie Marie wrote a poem that was included into her program. Her daughter my cousin Nichole also wrote a note and my auntie Beth wrote a note to her daughter. Once we had everything together for her program. My cousin Simone had her husband at that time print up the magazine style programs for free. And within a few days Simone returned to my auntie Beth's house with a bundle of finished programs.

Chapter 77 'The Family Cars Are Outside'

Since the programs were done. I had to find myself something else to do. So, I just drowned myself into everything involving her viewing. Now during that time my cousin Tina kept telling me that I needed to get some slept, because I hadn't really sleep since she had passed. I kept downplaying it, telling Tina 'I'm fine, I'll be okay,' but I really wasn't. I had spent several nights in a role over my auntie Beth's house.

It's the day before her viewing when I drove home to get myself something to wear for both the viewing and funeral. I got my brown suit and black slacks and dress shoes. Once back at my auntie's house I'm asked, 'did you get everything that you needed?' 'I believe I did but I'm not looking forward to tomorrow, me either, Sergio.'

On the day of the viewing I'm taking my time getting ready and after getting dressed. And when it was time to leave, I asked my auntie 'do you want to ride with me?' 'No, I'm riding with your aunties' 'okay' as I reluctantly got into my truck and drove to the funeral home. While driving I'm crying as I'm thinking about what I'm about to see. Once I arrived in the parking lot of the funeral home. I noticed that none of my family was there yet, so I waited. After about ten minutes they started arriving, so I got out of my truck and walked over and started speaking with some of them. Then after a few more family members arrived. We all walked into the funeral home together. I'm telling myself to just get through this, as I walked into the funeral home.

Once inside of the funeral home and when I entered into the room where her viewing was being held. I'm walking really slowly towards the front and I found myself a seat. Once seated I started looking around the room and everything looked beautiful. I'm crying but I'm trying to pull myself together. While seating there I saw several family members and friends of my sister get up and view her body. I sat there for a while. Until I mustered up enough courage to get up and I slowly walked up to the front to view my sister. And the closer I got to the casket. The more my tears would run down my face. Then once in front of the casket as I'm staring in disbelief. I noticed that her complexion appeared to be a lot darker then when she had passed. And after about ten minutes. I walked all the way to the back of the room and I sat in the last roll of pews. With nothing but me and my tears.

And after a few hours the viewing was finally over. And I hurried out of that funeral home. Once in my truck I started crying out loud for several minutes. Then I drove to my auntie Beth house and once in front of the house. I waited for my auntie to arrive. And when she arrived with several family members. Once inside my aunties appeared to surround my auntie Beth. And with me being a parent and a grandfather now I can really appreciate that, because I couldn't imagine what she had to be feeling at that time. And that night I spent the night over my auntie Beth house along with several of my other aunties. I sat up on the couch most of that night not really getting any sleep, as I'm really not looking forward to tomorrow.

The morning of the funeral my auntie Beth was getting dressed, as I just sat on the couch. Once she was dressed, she said, 'you need to hurry up and get dressed, Sergio.' I reluctantly got up and went into the bathroom. After my shower I cracked the door and asked, 'can you bring me my suit please?' 'Yes,' as she put the hanger onto the doorknob. When I heard that she had placed it onto the doorknob. I grabbed my suit and started getting dressed. Once dressed I came out of the bathroom and saw several of my family members were already there.

Then shortly after my auntie Beth said 'the family cars are out there', as we all got up and went outside. And I got into one of the Cadillac limos with my auntie Beth and some of my others auntie. I remember that being a very quite ride to the funeral home.

Chapter 78 'I Like That Idea'

Once inside I'm sitting near the front of the funeral. So, I could see her in the casket, and I began crying. At the beginning of the service family and friends got up to view her body again. I unwilling walked very slowly towards the casket with tears in my eyes as I stood there praying. Then I walked back to my seat and I couldn't believe how many people were there; it was standing room only. While I'm walking back to my seat. My Cousin Tina came up to me and put her arm around me and we walked back to my seat. Tina sat with me throughout the rest of the service. After the preacher was done speaking and they closed the casket. And the crying throughout the service just seemed to get amplified. Then the preacher asked for people to come up and say a few words. I really wanted to get up and speak but I knew I wasn't in any condition. And after everyone spoke, the preacher asked for the pallbearers to come forward.

I was one of six pallbearers, so I stepped forward. I was given a pair of white gloves and instructed on how to pick up and carry the casket into the Hurst, that's outside of the door. Once we got the casket into the Hurst, everyone inside of the funeral home began to exit. And the funeral flags were being placed onto the cars, as they lined up. I got back into the limo and I waited about twenty minutes. The cars were lined up for the funeral procession. Then all the cars followed the Hurst to the cemetery.

Once at the cemetery, all of the pallbearers carried the casket to the grave site. Then we placed the casket on top of a machine that lowered the casket into the ground. The preacher said a few words, as we all gathered around and cried. After the preacher said a few more words. They lowered the casket into the ground and as the casket lowered. People started walking towards their cars but I stood there until the casket was completely in the ground. Then I got back into the limo and we drove back to my aunties house.

Now the day of the viewing my auntie had mentioned that she wanted to have a reception at the house, but she didn't have enough tables and chairs. So I suggested 'we could just rent some tables and chairs'. 'That's true, but I don't have the room at the house Sergio'. 'We could rent some tents and have the reception in the back yard'. 'I like that idea Sergio'. 'I'll get on the telephone and find a place to rent everything that we need'. So I called around and I found a Rental Place in RedFord Michigan. I explained to the guy what I wanted to do and after he recommended options. I rented two twenty foot tents and eight long banquet tables and hundred seventy five chairs. I'm told that I would need to put a deposit on my order and I'm all set, so I drove up there. Once there I paid the deposit and was told 'everything will be delivered for you tomorrow morning'. When I got back to my aunties house, I told her that everything that I rented. 'And they'll be delivering it the morning of the funeral, so all we need now is some food'. 'I'll handle that Sergio'.

So after getting back from the cemetery. I told my auntie 'I'm going back up to the cemetery because I wanted to make sure that everything was everything'. 'Okay, but be careful Sergio'. 'I will' and I drove back up to the cemetery. And when I got there everyone was gone, so I got out of my truck and walked over towards her grave site. Once there I just stood around and checked my surroundings and everything seemed normal. So I walked back towards my truck. And I'm no were near soft dirt, and as I'm walking my right foot just sunk into the ground up to my knee.

Chapter 79 I Just Don't Understand

I struggled to get my foot loose. It was only when I yelled 'Pee Wee I'm not ready to go'. And only them was I able to remove my foot. Once I got back to my aunties house. I told her about what happen at the cemetery and she started laughing. And said, 'that was just your sister having some fun with you boy'.

Then about an hour later a delivery truck arrived, as they unloaded and set up everything in the backyard. My auntie didn't have to cook because most of my family brought over some food, ice, water and pop. I placed 4 plastic trash cans near each tent, and I put a garbage bag inside of the cans. Then I filled each one of them up with ice and several bottles of water and cans of pop.

Then after about thirty minutes everything was set up and people arrived. The weather was perfect, maybe around 75 degrees and sunny. And people would go into the house and after getting a plate. They would return to the backyard and have a seat under a tent. I was really surprised by how many people came. Sometimes, every chair in the backyard was filled. It went a lot better than I could've hoped. I was surprised when Tamil came over to give me her condolences and then she left. A lot of my sister's friends and co-workers that came to the funeral also came to the reception. I kept trying to stay busy because I knew that shortly everything would be over. And I would be forced to deal with my grief. While everyone seemed to be having a good time, I remember walking way into the back of the backyard. And I looked up into the sky and said, 'this is all for you, Pee Wee I really hope I'm doing everything the way that you wanted.' In her note and in person she asked me to look after her mother when she's gone. I told her, 'you don't have to ask me that I would've done that regardless she's family.'

After some hours people began to leave, and I started cleaning up and getting everything together. So when the rental company came, everything was all ready for pick up. After they picked everything up, I stayed outside and spoke with members of my family. Then I went into my sister's bedroom and I'm looking around and I couldn't believe that she still had every stuffed animal that I ever gave her over the years. While seating on her bed I'm crying as everything I looked at brought back memories. I wiped my face and went into the bathroom. Because I wanted to get my crying done before walking back into the living room with my auntie Beth. I knew if she saw me crying, she would start crying and I didn't want that to happen. After a while I eventually went home.

On my drive home, I'm crying. Once home, I went into the shower and cried. Then I went into my bedroom and laid across my bed and I cried myself to sleep. I woke up around three am. and I cried myself back to sleep. I repeated that same routine for several days. I just stayed home and cried until Monday.

Once I got back to work, I had to put on my "I'm good face". I had co-workers giving me their condolences which was nice of them, but I couldn't wait to complete my shift, so I could cry alone in my truck. Once my shift was finally over and I got into my truck. And while driving home, I started crying. Once home, I cried and when I got into the shower, I cried. When I got into my bed, I cried myself to sleep. At that time and even now, I just don't understand how someone at thirty years of age could die from breast cancer and she didn't smoke. She was very active playing softball a lot, so I'll just have to ask God 'why'?

Then shortly after that, I had to start packing to move again, but this time I won't be staying alone. I'll be moving into an apartment with Marie. Once we decided to live together, we started looking online at different apartments. We had narrowed our search between two apartments. The first apartment was in Westland, Michigan. The other apartment was in Northville Michigan. They're both two bedroom apartments, but the one in Northville had a bigger floor plan. We visited both places in person. The one in Westland was having a special that made the two bedrooms $750 a month, so I grabbed the paper of the special. And after looking at the apartment, we went to look at the apartment in Northville. And there was an attractive young lady that showed us the apartment.

Chapter 80 'But I Have A Girlfriend'

After showing us the apartment. We all went back into the leasing office. Once we were seated, she started going over the amenities of the apartment and asked, 'do you guys have any questions?' I said, 'yes, what's the monthly rate?' And she looked at the paperwork on her desk and said 'with the specials we're offering the monthly rent would be $ 1000 a month. But if you can find an apartment with these amenities that's cheaper, I'll match that price?' That's when I pulled out the special from the last apartment and said, 'we already have', as I handed her the special from the other apartment. 'That apartment is offering the same thing but is only $ 750 a month' as she looked over the paper. Then said, 'I'll match that price if you take it'. I was surprised when she said that because that special didn't offer the same things. I looked at Marie and she said 'yes' so I told the young lady 'we'll take it', as I shook her hand and stood up. And Marie got up and walked out of the office to go start her car. While I'm walking out of the office. The young lady grabbed my hand and placed a piece of paper into my hand. That read 'call me' with a phone number. I told her 'but I have a girlfriend' and she interrupted me and said 'I know, that's fine just hit me up, and I know where you live now'. While in disbelief but flattered as I walked out of the office.

Once outside, I tossed the number into the bushes. Then I got into the car and I never told Marie. Maybe a week or so later I was outside, and I overheard one of the landscaping guys mention. How he hated that 'PYT in the office got fired', so I assumed it was the young lady that showed us the apartment. And because of her matching that special.

And after about a week or so of moving, we're all moved in and the apartment was nice. It had over 1300 square feet with two bedrooms and two bathrooms. A large living room with a fireplace and the living room was connected to the dining room. And in the dining room, there were French doors that opened onto a patio. There also was a laundry room with a washer and dryer that was included. There was a small but see through kitchen. And the outside of the apartment was surrounded by a wooded area. The apartment seemed to be more of a townhouse than an apartment. And at first, everything was good. I'm was still working at Chrysler and Marie was working at a popular insurance company.

Then she had decided that she wanted to further her education, so she attended Phoenix University. And I didn't have a problem with that although we would argue sometimes about her schooling. Only because sometimes, I wanted her to go somewhere or do something with me and my children. And she would say that she had a class, or she had to study. And after a while we started arguing a lot about different things. Then I had developed a born spur in my right heel, and I wasn't able to work for a couple of months. And while on medical leave from work. I hadn't received my medical payments yet, so we argued even more about me not having my half towards the bills. While being frustrated with myself for not providing my share. And at that time, I felt that all I could do was to argue and fuse. And once I did receive my medical back pay. I paid her some but not what I owed.

And the week that I returned to work. My Union Rep. told me about 150 people with lower seniority then I had already lost their jobs. And how I should consider excepting the buyout. Now before going out on my medical leave. I heard rumors about layoffs and buyouts. While trying to decide on whether I should or shouldn't accept the buyout. And that was something that I should've discussed with Marie, but I didn't. Because we were so beefed out from arguing, I chose not to discuss that with Marie. And I eventually decided to accept the buyout and I never told Marie. My last day at Chrysler was in July of 2007. And about a week later, I received a check in the mail for a little over 50,000. I was excited and I cashed that check at the bank near the apartment. The bank wanted me to start a savings account, but I chose to just get it in cash.

Chapter 81 I Was Feeling Myself

After counting the money at the bank. Once home, I went into my bedroom and I counted again. I took a few thousand out and placed the rest of the money inside of a small unplugged fridge that was in our walk-in closet.

I had spoken to a few of the guys that I once hustled with about investing some of my money. And I was told that I'll get double my money back in a few weeks, so I invested. And I doubled my investment within two weeks, so I decided to do that again, but unfortunately, this time I didn't get anything back, so I thought they might've pocketed my money. But after inquiring and doing some investigating of my own. I discovered that everyone that invested had also taken a loss. So after that significant loss, I felt that I had to do something to try to make my money back. And the only sure way I knew of to make that much money back was to hustle. So I bought myself some powder cocaine and ten pounds of marijuana.

Once I cooked up some of the powder into crack. I hustled the rocks and sold the rest of the powder. And I fronted a few guys several pounds and I hustled the rest. And while looking back on that situation now. I didn't make the best of choices. Although I had what I felt was good intentions, but I didn't execute them properly. And at that time, I was sorta feeling myself. I had money drugs and guns and I was right back to hustling again. And I wasn't acting like myself. I was hanging out at clubs a lot and that wasn't something that I did. And looking back on that now. I was acting like some extravagant drug dealer witch I wasn't.

Chapter 82 5:16 pm

I wanted to make money. While promoting my music and hanging out, so I decided to throw parties. At this club called The Safari on Telegraph road between 5 and 6-mile roads in RedFord Michigan. I would throw parties there once a month for several months. And I would always get into arguments with Marie about not inviting her and I would say 'it's not your kind of party' which I felt was true. But I also just wanted to handout and flirt if I chose without worrying about her being there. I would give away samples of my latest music CD and music t-shirt at the door. And some days I would make money but most days I would be lucky to break even. But I always would have a good time with some family and a bunch of people and a few friends.

But as I look back on that situation now. It was more about me partying and handing out then business because I wasn't making any money. I was just smoking and drinking a lot, so much so. That a few times I didn't even come home. I would be too blowed to drive home. That I would get a room near the party. Then I would call Marie and tell her that I'm sleeping on my cousin Nichole's couch. And I wasn't always the best boyfriend on those nights. Then I finally woke up and realized that I wasn't making any money. So I stopped given the parties and got myself a job.

After applying I got a job near our apartment. Where I was building small power tools by hand. Then one day shortly after getting that job my cell phone rings. And when I answer it was my x wife Tamil and I'm asked, 'are you sitting down Sergio?' 'Yes why?' as I was sounding nervous because I thought that something was wrong with our children. So I said 'please just tell me what is it please', as I'm sounding aggravated. And she said, 'your grandmother just called hear looking for you'. 'But she has my cell phone number, so she could've called me'. 'I don't know about that, but she said that your father is in hospice and he's dying', as I got really quite in my disbelief. Then she said, 'did you hear what I said Sergio?' 'Yeah, I heard you'. 'Now I know you're not close to your father, but promise me that you'll at least call him please?' 'I'll call you back, but thank you for calling. I was worried that it was something pertaining to our children'. 'No, there fine but find out about your father please?' 'I will but I'll call you back. I'm about to call my Grandmother'. After getting off the telephone, I called my grandmother and I asked, 'where's my father?' 'He's in hospice in Ann Arbor', as I'm giving the address. Once off the telephone, I walked over to my supervisor and I explained my situation. And I'm told that I could leave, so I got into my van and drove to the hospice place in Ann Arbor Michigan.

After about forty five minutes, I'm at the hospice place. Once inside, I walked up to the front desk where I told the receptionist my father's name and I'm asked to sign in please. Once I finished sighing my name, she told me his room number, as she pointed towards the direction of his room. I walked down the hallway towards his room. Once I reached the outside of his room. I stood there for a few minutes to gather myself because I didn't know what to expect. Then I took a deep breath and nervously entered the room.

Once inside, I saw my father and Jane, both looking shocked to see me. I saw him lying in a bed that was in front of me. And his girlfriend Jane was sitting in a chair on the other side of his bed. Now I haven't seen my father in many years, so as I'm walking towards his bed. Jane got up and walked over towards me and whispered, 'he has cancer' and walked back to her seat. I walked around the bed and I sat in a chair that was near my father's right side. Then he asked, 'how are you doing'? As if he wasn't sick in hospice and I said, 'I'm good', as we started talking.

After a while I asked him, 'why haven't I seen or heard from you in many years?' He wouldn't answer my question, he would just change the subject. So it became painfully obvious that he wouldn't answer so I stopped asking. Although I would've liked some answers, but I just felt that this wasn't the time to be asking.

The first day I was up there visiting for more than six hours. Then on my drive home, I called my job to make sure that I'll be able to take some time off from work. The next day I went back up there and I stayed for about eight hours. I was up there visiting for several days in a role. Anywhere between eight and ten hours per visit. After a few visits, he told me that he had cancer, but he didn't say what kind. And during a visit, he notices me looking at his legs. I'm told 'there retaining water that's why they're so big and hard touch my leg', so I reached over to touch his leg and it felt hard like cement. I've never cared for Jane and she was there every time that I visited.

On day six of me visiting my father. Jane was on the telephone talking to I'm assuming her sister that lives in California. And she's bragging on how much money she will get once my father has died. Now he was asleep but I'm in the room. And I could hear her, and I became so frustrated. That I got up and walked out of the room to keep from physically hurting her. And after about thirty minutes. I came back into the room and she's no longer on the telephone. And my father was awake, so we spoke for a few more hours. Then I said, 'I'll be back up here tomorrow ', as I walked out of the door.

Only to return the following morning. And when I entered into the room. They were already discussing his retirement and Jane said, 'I have the papers here', as she held up the papers. And after a few hours, he fell asleep, so I walked out to get some water. And when I returned into the room, she said, 'watch this', as Jane sighed my father's name to the retirement papers. Then she walked over to me and showed me how well she had forged his signature. And when I saw the signature. I knew that she had done that before and then she bragged about doing it. And that just pissed me off so I walked out of the room again. Because I wanted to keep from whooping her ass, and when I walked back into the room. He was awake, so we talked. Then he said whatever you do once I'm gone, Jane make sure that you take care of my Son, and my Twin Brother okay'? And she said 'I will' I stayed a little longer than I left. And while driving home, I'm thinking about everything that I've seen and heard.

And the next day while visiting my uncle Allen (my father's brother) came into the room with grandmother (my father's mother). I noticed that whenever my uncle and grandmother were in the room, Jane wasn't. After they left while speaking with my father. He asked me to do him a favor, so I asked, 'what is it?' 'I need for you to look after Jane once I'm gone'. I hesitated in my response as I thought about everything and I reluctantly said, 'I will'

The next morning I arrived around eleven am and my reason for coming up early was because I wanted to leave earlier. And when I got into the room. I noticed that he wasn't looking so good, but I didn't say anything. And I visited with him for about five hours. Then I told him 'get some rest and I'll be back up here tomorrow ', as I leave out of the room. While driving home on the freeway. My cell phone rings and when I answered it's Jane telling me 'you need to come back up here now it's not looking good for your father. So I turned back around. And once back inside of the room. I looked at the clock on the wall and it's 5 pm. And he was doing what I know now to be the gargle of death. So when I heard that, I went and got his nurse. Once the nurse entered the room with me, I asked, 'how long does that last?' 'This could last several hours or days it just depends'. Then I asked the nurse, 'could you increase his morphine?' 'I can't, but I can call his doctor and ask'. 'Can you call and ask him for me now please. Because this isn't going to last hours or days but minutes'. The nurse leaves then returns telling me 'the doctor has approved the increase' and she walked around his bed to increase his morphine. Once done, I asked her, 'he's not feeling anything now right?' 'Not after that increase', as she leaves out of the room. I looked at the clock and it was 5:12 pm. And he stopped gargling and passed away at 5:16 pm. I reached over and closed his eyes, as Jane just stood there crying. Then Jane took off his favorite gold watch he got for working so many years at Ford Motor Company. And she also got a black switch blade that he had up there, and she handed them to me.

Chapter 83 'The Great Resection'

I stayed for a few minutes and as I was about to leave. 'I'm so glad that you were here Sergio I didn't know what to do, so thank you'. 'I didn't know what to do either I just did what I felt was best for my father', as I walked out of the door.

While driving home, I had tears running down my face. Which, I thought, was surprising because I wasn't that close to him. And a few days before he passed, I told him whenever the time came. I would do whatever I could to make sure that he wasn't in any pain.

Then a few days later after he passed, I got a telephone call from Jane. And she told me that she's in the hospital and could I come up there. I didn't want to go but I thought about what my father asked, so I reluctantly went.

Once I got to the hospital, I asked the receptionist what room was she in, as I'm told. Then I walked towards her room. Once I entered the room. I saw that Jane was sitting up in the bed and she's covered in bruises. So I asked 'what happen?' 'I fell down some stairs at the house'. 'How?' 'I had been drinking again'. And once she said that it made sense because she's always had a drinking problem. I visited with her for maybe about an hour. Then as I was about to walk out of the room, she asked, 'can you come back up tomorrow', and I didn't respond. 'And when you come tomorrow, can you bring me some snacks and crossword puzzles'? I'm thinking to myself as she's asking this bitch got me coming back tomorrow and she wants me to bring her snacks and puzzles. But reluctantly I agreed.

The next day I went to the hospital with snacks and crossword puzzles. I stayed for maybe an hour and then I left the hospital. And once home, I told myself that I'm not going back up to that hospital anymore. She's not my mother and I don't even like her. Then after a few days, my cell phone rang and when I answered it was the hospital. And a nurse told me about Jane pulling out her catheter and that she gave me your number to call. And how one minute she's screaming and then she's crying, so could you please come up and help her to settle down please'? 'I'll be there in about an hour'. 'Thank you'. And once off the cellphone, I'm thinking about how this bitch is finding ways for me to come up there, as I got dressed.

Once I entered her room and she seemed to be fine. So I asked 'what's going on, why is a nurse calling me?' And she said 'you hadn't been up in a few days and I didn't think that you would come if I called, so did you bring me anything?' 'No, I didn't and I'm only here because a nurse asked me to'. 'I'll be going home in a few days' 'that's great you take care of yourself ', as I leave out of the room. As I'm walking to my van I'm talking to myself about how this bitch has been using me but I can't change the past.

Once home, I decided to clean up my apartment because I'm upset. And I hoped that would've help me to get rid of some of my frustration, but it didn't work. So I just rolled up a blunt and smoked and wrote.

After a few days my cell phone ring and it's Jane. 'I'm out of the hospital now'. 'That's good I'm glad that you're out but I'm kinda busy right now, so I'll call you back okay?' 'Okay, now, but call me back please'. 'I will but not until later because I'm really busy', as I hung up my cell phone. Then later that evening my cell phone rings and it's Jane again, so when I answered she said 'I can't sleep and you sound like your father Sergio, so I was hoping that you would talk with me until I'm able to fall asleep?' Now mind you, I don't think I sound anything like my father. Other then we both have deep voices. I, unfortunately, spoke with her for about twenty minutes and then I hung up the telephone. And I'm thinking to myself, why am I doing all of this for her I need to bring this to an end somehow.

The next day she called again and told me, 'I think your father would want you to have his truck. So I want to give it to you, so do you want it?' He had a newer Black Ford Expedition, so I told her 'Sure I'll gladly take his truck'. I don't need it I have a new truck already. I think you should get his truck and you are his only child, so I'll set that up. Now there may be some Probate Court stuff to deal with first, but don't worry about that stuff I'll take care of it Sergio'. 'Thank you for giving me something of my fathers'. 'No problem Sergio'. Now my father had a massive gun collection, so I asked, 'what are you doing with his guns?' 'I don't know yet', as she quickly changed the subject and started telling me that they were married. Now knowing my father, I just didn't see him marrying her. I mean she's always been very dependent on him, so I didn't believe that to be true. Plus unfortunately, he was somewhat of a male chauvinist, so I'm sure that he was messing around on her, as he started messing around with her while married to my mother.

Then suddenly Jane stopped calling and at first, I thought that was great but after about a month. I decided to call Jane, but I got no answer or call back. I thought that was odd because she had been calling me several times a day for several weeks. Then after a few weeks of trying to call her with no answer, I got a letter from a Probate Layer in the mail. When I opened the letter and started reading. And as I'm reading things like "you don't get any of your father's estate. He didn't think that you were his son because he had testicular cancer, so with just one testicle, you may not be his son". And would I sigh this paper and mail it back please'. After reading that bullshit. I balled up that letter and threw it into the trash. That letter was my proof that she's been playing me the whole time.

A few weeks later, I got a telephone call from Jane. And she's asking me 'did you get a letter from the lawyer?' 'I did'. 'And did you sign the paper?' 'No, I didn't, and I won't sign that bullshit! And whatever your trying to do now won't work in the long run'. 'I don't know what you're talking about Sergio, but I'm going to get away with it,' and I just hung up my cell phone. Now I'm furious that she hasn't done anything that my father asked.

Then after a few days, I decided to drive out to my father's house in Ypsilanti Michigan. When I got down to his dirt road I just parked, as I watched people moving his things into a large moving truck. Then a few days later Jane called to tell me that she sold his house. And that she's taken his guns to the State Police to be melted. I'm also moving in with a sister in California. I'm not saying anything, as she's speaking. Once done speaking as she went to ask me something, but I just hung up my cell phone. I was so pissed that she hadn't done any of my father's last wishes. She had called me a few more times, but I never answered. I never called or saw her ever again. I heard that she had him cremated witch I didn't mind because he had expressed to me in the past that he wanted that. Although I didn't like the fact that she didn't have a funeral or service for him. So his mother and sibling could see him once again.

Then years later, I heard through the grapevine that Jane was having some health issues and wasn't doing well. And to be fair, I was happy to learn about that. Then years later, I learned that she had passed away. Now I don't wish death on anyone but when you do wrong, wrong things happen and some call that karma. I couldn't believe the drama I had dealt with. From my father's death and Janes bullshit.

Then a few months later I'm laid off, so now I'm looking for another job. But everywhere that I went to submit my resume. I was being told that I'm overqualified for that position because of me working at Chrysler, so no one wanted to hire me. In fact, during one job interview, I was told 'you're more than qualified for this job, but I don't want to hire you'. And I asked 'why?' 'Because by the time I got you trained. You would've found a new job that's pays you a lot more money. And I'll have to find a new person to hire and train all over again, so I'm sorry but I can't hire you'. And with the economy at that time being referred to as "The Great Resection". So after countless submissions of my resume. I couldn't find a job, so I called my uncle Mark that owns a construction company. And I asked him about some work. And was told 'you don't have any kind of license or certification to do this work alone. Your other uncle Damon has a work crew working for me right now. So ask him if you could work with him and let me know what he says'.

Chapter 84 Unemployment Insurance

I called my uncle Damon and I asked him if I could work with him. I'm told 'sure you'll be painting and doing drywall so would that be a problem?' 'No, it wouldn't' as I'm told where to meet him in the morning.

The next morning when I arrived at the Inkster Projects, that was being renovated. My uncle Damon told me what he wanted me to do and I saw some of my brothers working with him also. After getting a check for that week of work. We're my uncle Damon would cash and pay me in cash. After working with him for maybe a month or so, I became a working supervisor. Where I would work some and I would gather all the paperwork of jobs that we had done for that week. And I would take that information home and I would enter it into my laptop. And I would print it out with the prices that my uncle would charged. And my uncle Damon would take it to my uncle Mark. So we could get paid for that week of work.

That job was good for awhile, but then I noticed how the work was slowing down. So I told my uncle and brothers that this work will be ending soon. And I worked for him for maybe six more months, then I quit. And maybe a few months after I quit, all the work had dried up, as I predicted.

Once I stopped working for my uncle. I collected my unemployment insurance. From my former job that had laid me off. I got 52 weeks of benefits at first. Then the president had extended the benefits, so I got another 26 weeks. Then I received a letter saying I qualified for a bridge card. So I went to the nearest Social Service Office near me, and after filling out the application. I'm told to check my mailbox in about a few weeks. And after a month, I received my bridge card in the mail, and I received 199 dollars a month. So now I'm able to buy food with my card, but before getting that card. I remember going to the grocery store and buying a week worth of food with only seven dollars and some change. I got very little money with my unemployment checks. And there were a few times that I had to give blood for money to help pay some of my bills.

I also went from getting my children every other weekend to maybe once a month if that. It wasn't 'cause I didn't want to I just didn't have the money for gas. In order to get my children I would have to drive from my apartment in Wixom Michigan. To Detroit to get my oldest son and then to Belleville, Michigan to get my other two children and back to my apartment.

Chapter 85 Ashamed And Embarrassed

After making that trip several times. I remember asking their mothers a few times if they could either pick up or drop off my children, but that never happened. So I was assuming that my children were looking at me, as the absentee dead beat father. I never told or would complain to anyone about how bad my situation had gotten. Even when asked, I would just tell them I'll be okay'. I was just too ashamed and embarrassed. I've always done for myself and if I couldn't get it, then I went without. I've never liked having to ask or depend on anyone for anything. I've always been a very prideful, and independent person before this happen to me. But since being in this nursing home for several years now. I've had to learn how to ask people for help and that's just something that I've always disliked.

Now all of my children played sports throughout high school and my daughter even had recitals where she would sing. And I made it to most if not all of my son's football games, but I only made it to a few of my daughter's basketball games and recitals. And that's something that I will always regret even now. And it wasn't because I didn't want to go, I just didn't have money for gas at those times.

I found myself feeling really depressed and even suicidal. I wasn't working so I'm not able to pay my bills, and I wasn't able to see or be with my children. And I just wasn't liking where I was in my life. Then after feeling depressed for the longest time, I manage to shake off my suicidal thoughts. And I began sending out my resume again. And whenever I could afford, I would purchase myself a half-ounce of marijuana. And I would smoke some and sell the rest only for gas money and groceries as I waited on a job response.

Then after a few weeks with no responses to my resume. I walk across the street to a temp service. Where I applied for a job and after a few days. I got a telephone call offering me a job at a detergent factory near my apartment.

I accepted the job and I was to start on Monday. Then on Monday, I walked into the building and was shown what to do. And after eight hours, I leave and go back home. The next morning, I wasn't feeling so good, but I didn't want to call off because I had just started, so I went in anyway.

Chapter 86 A 2% Chance

Then on a Tuesday, August 10th, 2010. I went into work and it was a very hot day outside. Once inside, it was even hotter, as I'm told to work in the back. So I walked to the back of the building with no visible fan insight. And I'm unloading ten pound boxes. Then I'm moved to another job and after a while I'm moved again.

Now it's break time, so I walked over to the other side of the building. And I arrived at the break area and sat at the wooden pic-nick table. Where I ate my lunch. And after thirty minutes. I walked back to the job and continued unloading ten pound buckets of laundry detergent onto a wooden pallet that's on the floor. Then I'm told that I just suddenly passed out onto the concrete floor. And I'm told that the ambulance was called and once on the stretcher. I'm placed inside of the ambulance. And I was told that I had a temperature of 105.7 and that I died in the ambulance. We're the EMT performed CPR on me as I'm rushed to the nearest hospital.

Which was Novi Providence Hospital in Novi, Michigan. I'm brought into the hospital while in a coma. And at that time, I weighed around 425 pounds. While in my coma, most of my organs had failed. I was on life support and do to my liver and kidneys failure. My body was retaining fluid, so I gained another 150 pounds. I was told I was so bloated that they couldn't get me into the EKG machine. I wasn't urinating or having any bowl movements. And that lasted for almost two weeks. I had three ulcers that burst inside of my stomach. I also had developed yellow joneses, so I had a yellow puss just seeping out of my pores. And both of my eyes were bloodshot red because they had hemorrhaged. I was told that I looked possessed. And I was only given a 2% chance to survive. The doctors were scrambling to discover what happened. And my mother was told on several occasions by doctors. If I did survive, I would be brain dead and remain in a vegetated state for life.

Chapter 87 2 Guys Arrived

Almost two weeks later, I started urinating. And my family was notified of my small improvement. Then I started having bowel movements, so that meant that my kidneys and liver are now working again. Then after receiving the last antibiotic in the whole hospital. The doctors told my family, 'if that last antibiotic doesn't work, there's nothing else that we can do for him. So we just have to wait and hope it works'. My X girlfriend Marie discovered me being hospitalized a day after being rushed to the hospital. There were several members of my family and Marie at the hospital almost every day. I remained in a coma for more than thee months. With doctors and specialists telling my family every other day, 'it's not looking good or he's doing better today'. I can only imagine the emotional roller coaster that my children and family had to deal with at that time.

Then with no one stepping up, Marie took it upon herself and became my legal guardian. And she arraigned for me to get medical and disability insurance. She along with some family, helped to pay my rent at my apartment for several months. And when she could no longer afford to pay my rent anymore. She got with her mother and a few friends and they moved my things into a storage unit. And she paid my storage rent for many years alone.

While in my coma, I had several vivid dreams that were like movies. What I found to be ironic in every one of my dreams I was in a hospital. In one of my many dreams, I was in the hospital for something. And my left leg got amputated from the knee down. In another dream, I was in a hospital that's connected to a Casio in Canada. I don't know why I was in hospital but two of my aunties and my mother worked there. My mother appeared to be a housekeeper. And she would come to my door at times and I would plead with her to help me to escape. One thing that I fount strange and even odd now. That I was able to say a short prayer while in my coma.

Then on what I believe to be December 1, 2010, I awoke from my comma. And I looked around the room and I realized that I was in a hospital. But I didn't know if that was just another dream. And I'm trying to remember what happened to me because I was just at work and now, I'm in a hospital. As I'm looking around the room, I looked down at my chest and I seen several wires that are connected to a machine. Then I looked around the room some more and I realized that I couldn't move anything, but my eyes and I couldn't speak. I counted seventeen different machines that I could see that was hooked up to me somehow. Then after a while a nurse walked into the room and I tried to speak but I couldn't. So, I just followed her with my eyes. And once she noticed that my eyes were following her, she ran out of the room.

And after about five minutes, she returned with several doctors. And they asked me many questions, but I couldn't speak or move. Then a doctor noticed that I couldn't speak, so I'm asked too 'blink once for yes and twice for no please'. So I'm blinking to answer several of there questions. Once done, I'm told 'we're going to notify your family about this', as they walked out of the room.

Once they left the room, I began to cry, as I'm trying to figure out what the hell happen to me. Then as I'm looking around the room. I noticed a feeding tube that was next to my bed and placed inside of my nose. And after a while I seen my mother walk into the room. I couldn't speak so I just cried as she wiped my tears and said, 'I always knew that you would wake up', as she placed her hand on my forehead.

Then after a few weeks, I'm moved into a private room. Where people can visit with me, but I'm still not able to speak or move. So, I just laid there as my family and some friends would visit. And do to my eyes' having hemorrhaged. I got three eye drops that I would receive three times a day for several weeks. I'm not a diabetic but I would get my finger poked to check my sugar three times a day for several weeks.

Then I'm moved again into a bigger private room that had a full bathroom. And Marie would be with me at the hospital almost every day. And after leaving the hospital for work only to return back to the hospital. She even brought her electronic blanket and curling irons so whenever she would spend the night on the couch/day bed. And after taking a shower and changing her clothes she could curl her hair before leaving out for work. Once done, she would kiss me on my forehead and would say, 'I'll be back after work,' and she would leave. My mother doesn't drive so she would get dropped off at the hospital. And she would be there for several weeks at a time. I was very fortunate to be able to have someone with me for almost 24 hours. On nights that Marie wasn't there, my mother would be there.

I still couldn't speak so Marie had written down the alphabet on some small pieces of paper. That way I could try to spell out whatever I was trying to say. But after several weeks, I began to be able to whisper. Now while being in my coma, I had developed a very large pressure wound that was located on my backside in my tail bone area. I learned that I got that wound because I wasn't being turned while in my coma. At first, my wound was the actual length of my forearm.

I was told by Marie that she could see my spine whenever they would do my wound treatment. Once they learned of my wound, I started receiving a wound treatment every day. And at first, they would pack my wound with four whole rolls of gauze and then cover it with a dressing. One day while doing my treatment after being placed onto my side. I heard the doctor that was doing my treatment gasp, so when I heard that, I asked, 'what's wrong'? And I'm told that a piece of my tail bone came out. Then after my treatment was completed and I was placed back onto my back. I looked over towards Marie and seen that she had tears in her eyes. I was able to speak somewhat but my words weren't being pronounced properly. I knew that having a trachea wasn't helping. But then I discovered that some of my front teeth had been removed. I was told that happen when they were trying to put the feeding tube into my mouth but couldn't. Now those teeth were already loose, so I wasn't mad. But I'm not trying to smile at anyone directly.

It was a few days before Christmas in 2010. When over thirty plus members of my family crammed into my room to visit. I was shocked that they came and all at once. It was also very emotional for me, as I cried after they left.

And whenever Marie would visit, she would always leave out of my room to go eat. After a few days of noticing, I asked, 'why do you leave out to eat?' 'I don't want to eat in front of you knowing that you can't eat'. 'That's nice of you, but you don't have to keep doing that I'll be okay'. With me haven that feeding tube I haven't eaten or drunk anything in several months. After a while, I started asking Marie to give me some crushed ice in my mouth, please?' 'No, I'm sorry you can't have anything to drink'. And after several days of asking Marie finally went to get me some crushed ice. Once back in my room as she would pour some ice chips into my mouth. And I didn't chock so I started asking her for crushed ice several times a day.

Once while visiting Marie had a sucker and it looked to taste really good, so I asked if I could have some? Marie put the sucker into my mouth, and everything seemed to be okay until I started chocking. Then in a hurry, she placed her whole hand into my mouth to retrieve the sucker. While scratching the roof of my mouth, as she pulled her hand back and got that sucker. Once she was done, I started laughing. And she said 'that shit isn't funny Sergio. I'll be damn you go through all of this to live only to die from choking on a sucker that you're not supposed to have and that I gave you!'

About a week later, a lady came into my room and she said, 'I'm here to perform a swallow test on you'. And I asked, 'what's that?' After explaining what it was, she put some crushed ice into my mouth with a plastic spoon, as I swallowed without any complications. Then I was told 'you passed that test, but I have a few more tests for you to take. And once you've pass every test, you'll be able to get rid of that feeding tube and eat and drink again, so I'll be back tomorrow', as she leaves.

The next day she returned but this time she had some Jello. 'This is soft, but I want to see if you can swallow this,' as she put a spoonful into my mouth. After swallowing, I asked 'if I could have some more please', as she feeds me the rest of the Jello. After a few more days of taking her test, I'm told that you've passed and once this feeding tube is taken out, you'll be able to eat and drink again'.

After a few weeks, the feeding tube was taken out. And after five plus months of not being able to eat or drink, I'm finally able. And the first meal I had to eat was some Chinese food that Marie got. And that was delicious, I think almost anything would've tasted good at that time. Then my auntie Dana brought three large bags of home-cooked food up to the hospital. I was surprised to see her. And really surprised that she brought some food. There was so much food that we ate for several days. Marie would make us a plate and warm up the plates in the hospitals' microwave. Then after feeding me, she would put the leftovers into the hospital's refrigerator until it was all eaten.

It was on January 31st, 2011 the night before my birthday. It was late so I told Marie that I'm going asleep. The following morning when I awoke. I seen a huge happy birthday banner taped to the wall at the foot of my bed. And as I looked around the room. All I seen was smaller happy 40th birthday banners. And she also had gotten me a birthday cake with paper plates and forks. I was so amazed, and I asked her, 'how and when were you able to do all of this?' 'I just made the time Sergio', as she cut and feed me a piece of the cake. The fact that she did that for me on top of everything else that she's done and continues to do for me even now. I was and will forever be grateful and thankful and always appreciative of here!

Then on February the 3rd 2011 a doctor came into my room and he told me and Marie 'we'll be releasing him soon'. And Marie said, 'I want to go look at some nursing homes in person before he's released'. 'That's fine. Just let us know, so we'll know where to send him', as Marie agreed and he leaves. 'Now, I need to find you a nursing home that takes your insurance and can handle your wound and trachea'. A few days later, while she was visiting, I asked Marie 'any luck yet'. 'I've called around but I hadn't visited any nursing homes in person yet'.

Then on Monday, February 7th, 2011, I'm released. They called Marie while she was at work and told her that I'm being released now, 'but I haven't found him a nursing home yet'. 'Don't worry we've already selected one for him and they except his insurance'. 'Where is it?', as she's giving the information. 'When is he being released?' 'Right now there already on their way to pick him up'. Then less than an hour later two guys arrived with a stretcher to take me to the nursing home.

After a thirty five minute bumpy ride I arrived at AC Nursing Home, on the EastSide of Detroit Michigan. As I'm being rolled into the nursing home. I asked, 'are we in the basement?' 'No were on the first and only floor'. Then they stopped at the front desk and inquired about what room. Once told, I'm taken to the room that's very dark and the smell was horrible. As I'm placed into a bed that's up against the wall. Once they leave as I'm lying there just crying. Because I had a bad feeling about that nursing home. And I knew that I had to make the best of my situation.

Chapter 88 8:16 PM

After work, Marie came into my room at the new nursing home. And before sitting down, she said, 'I don't like this place' while pulling a chair near my bed. 'And just so you know Sergio I didn't pick this place for you', as she sits down. And I whispered, 'I don't like this place either'. 'And with me working and being at the hospital so much. I just haven't had the time to actually visit any nursing home'. I told her don't worry about it I'll be okay. I just need to hurry up and get better soon'. 'I'm going to get you out of here soon, Sergio; it's late, so I'm about to leaves but I'll be back up here tomorrow', as she kissed me on my forehead and leaves.

The following morning I'm given a breathing treatment and told 'you'll have to wear this for a few hours a day', as the nurse placed the mask onto my face. And after several hours, my nurse returned to remove the mask. The room that I was in was really dark. The only light I would get came from whenever my door was opened or cracked. Or when some sunshine would come through the blinds of a door that's in the back of my room.

Then later that day a wound nurse came in and said, 'I'm here to do your treatment', as she rolled me over onto my side towards the wall. Once done as I'm rolled back onto my back. And I'm told 'you really have a very large wound back there, so I'll be back tomorrow to do your treatment,' and she leaves. Then when a CENA came into the room I asked her if she could turn on my television, because I couldn't. Once she turned on my television, she placed the remote next to me in my bed as I'm smelling marijuana. I don't think that she knew that I was a total quadriplegic. I even smelled marijuana and liquor on other CENA'S and housekeepers.

Then after a couple of weeks. My mother had gotten a ride with my auntie Marie to visit me. And once inside my room as she was pulling up a chair near my bed. She asked, 'how are you doing?' And I whispered, 'I'm in a lot of pain'. 'Are the nurses given you something for your pain?' 'I don't know'. And she said, 'I'll be right back', as she walked out of the room. Once back in my room, she said, 'the nurse said you're receiving something for pain'. 'If I am, I can't tell I don't feel any different after taking my medication'. Then when she stood up and was about to leave. I saw her staring at my legs, so I asked, 'what is it mom?' And she said 'your right leg looks a lot bigger than your left leg. Then she said, 'maybe it's just me', as she leaves.

The next day when Marie came up to visit. I hadn't been washed up since being there so I asked Marie to wash me up. She agreed and leaves, and when she returned with soapy water and towels. Then she began washing me and when she got to my legs, she said 'your right leg is bigger than your left leg Sergio'. And I told her that my mother was saying the same thing yesterday. So once she was done washing me up, I'm told 'I'll be right back', as she walked towards the door. And I asked, 'where are you going?' 'I'm going to get a nurse to look at your leg', as she leaves out of my room. About ten minutes later she returned with my nurse and she pulled back the sheet to show my nurse my leg. She looked at my leg and told Marie 'his right leg isn't bigger', as Marie discussed with her that it is larger. And once the nurse leaves Marie said 'that's some bullshit Sergio your right leg is much bigger than your left leg'! And after Marie complained about my leg for several days. The nursing home had someone come out to perform an ultrasound on my leg. After he was done, I inquired about the results. And I was told that nothing was found.

Then one day while watching television, I somehow managed to slide down in my bed. So after about twenty minutes, I managed to hit my call light. Once my CENA arrived, I whispered, 'can I be pulled up in the bed please'. I'm told 'let me go get some help and I'll be right back', as she leaves. After about ten minutes, she returned with another female CENA. Once she explained what I wanted done. The CENA'S moved my bed away from the wall just enough, so one of them could get on that side of my bed. Then they both interlocked their arms undermine and begin to count. '1, 2, 3', as they yanked me up in the bed. So fast and hard that my catheter came out of my penis. The balloon that was inside of my bladder was literally between my legs.

And I screamed so loud, but you could barely hear me, as my tears just started flowing. The one CENA asked, 'what's wrong', as I pointed down between my legs. Once she realized what happen, I'm told 'I know that hurts', as I managed to say, 'what the hell do you think', as tears continued to run down my face. Then I'm told 'I'm going to go get your nurse,' and she leaves. After about five minutes, my nurse entered the room. With a new catheter to put back inside of me. I'm already in extreme pain as she inserted the new catheter. I screamed as she put it into me, but no sound came out, as I just gritted my teeth while in much pain. After that happened, I realized why I had a bad feeling about the nursing home in the beginning.

The next day when Marie came up to visit. I explained to her what happen yesterday. 'Wow are you serious I can't believe that shit. I really need to hurry up and get you out of here, so how's your pain now?' As I whispered, 'it's terrible'. 'I'm going to ask my boss if she knows of anything that can help with your pain'. Then we started talking and she said, 'have you noticed that I'm up here almost everyday?' 'Yeah, I have'. It's because I don't like this place and I'm so worried about you whenever I'm not here. That I just have to come up to see that you're okay'.

The next day after work when Marie came up, she told me that her boss said to try something called neuron tin. 'It's supposed to be good for nerve ending pain, so I'm going to tell your nurse and hopefully there able to get it for you, so I'll be back', as she leaves. Once back I'm told 'your insurance covers it, so they're going to order you some now and you should have it in a few days'. After a couple of days, while Marie was visiting. The medication arrived and my nurse gave me the medication. And within thirty minutes, my pain level went from a plus ten to a six level. Now that may not seem to be significant, but I have a very high threshold for pain, so for me, that's very significant. After taking the medication, I'm told, 'I can tell that it's working your no longer frowning like you were before'. 'It is, so tell your boss I said thank you for me please'.'I will I'm just glad that it's working and so quickly'. I had been in that nursing home for over a month and I hadn't received a bed bath or a shower. So, I'm still asking Marie to wash me up whenever she would come to visit me every couple of days.

Now it's around the first of March 2011. When my cousins Mark and his Brother Ron came to visit. Once they entered into the room, I could smell marijuana on them, but I didn't mind I used to smoke. And I was surprised and glad to see Mark because he lives in California. They gathered some chairs and once seated we started talking. Then my nurse at that time was a younger woman that walked into the room. And asked, 'do you need anything?' 'No, I'm good but thank you', as she slowly walked out of the room. 'Now y'all know the only reason she came in here was to check y'all outright', as we all started laughing. Then maybe an hour later my nurse walked back into my room again. And she tried to spark up a conversation with my cousins. But they were about to leave, so as there walking by my nurse said 'y'all sure do smell really good', as my cousins just laughed and told me 'we'll be back up to see you Cuz', as my nurse leave also. And within ten minutes, my nurse returned and asked me to call them back up here, so I can buy some weed from them'. Now mind you, I'm a total quadriplegic. I can't move and there isn't a telephone in my room, so I couldn't call if I wanted to anyway.

Now it was the second Wednesday of March in 2011. When I had a bowel movement and after several minutes. I manage to hit my call light around 8:16 pm. A nurse came into my room around 9:21 pm. I told her I had a BM and she reached over me and turned off and moved the call light out of my reach. And told me 'a wound nurse will be in here to clean you up tomorrow morning', as she leaves and closes the door. I'm shocked that she didn't do anything, and I can't move or yell for help, so I'm forced to lay in my fesses.

The next morning around 10:45 am a wound nurse came in and asked me, 'how long have you been waiting to be cleanedup'? 'Since last night', as I explained what happen. 'I can't believe this', as she cleaned me up and did my treatment. 'I just want to apologize to you for not being cleaned up last night', as she leaves. Then later that day the wound nurse came back into my room. And told me, 'you really need to go to the hospital now!' And I asked, 'is this because of me not being cleaned up last night?'

Chapter 89 Dead Skin

'I'm not supposed to say anything, but yes, your wound is extremely infected. If you don't go to the hospital now, you could die within a day or so. I've already called the ambulance', as she pleaded with me to go. 'I'll go but only back to the Novi Hospital'. 'That's where you're going'. Then I asked, 'can you call my guardian Marie and tell her what happen and where I'm going?' 'I will', as she leaves. After about thirty minutes transportation arrived. Once on the stretcher I'm taken back to the hospital.

Once in there I'm placed into a bed, as several IVs are placed into my arms. A doctor came into my room and said, 'it's a good thing that you came when you did, or you wouldn't be here'. And when Marie got there, she asked 'what happen Sergio. After explaining I'm told 'I can't believe that shit happen. I will make sure that you'll never go back to that shit whole', as her tears fell. I spent a week in the hospital. While taken multiple antibiotics and IVs. A few days before being released Marie came in and told me 'I've found you a new nursing home. I've been there and it looks to be clean and bright and they also take your insurance. They also can treat your wound unlike that hell hole that you were in, but always remember no nursing home will ever be perfect. There will always be problems.

Then on April 1st, 2011 I'm released and transported to the new nursing home. That I'll call Empire Nursing Homes in Dearborn Heights Michigan. Once I arrived on the stretcher as I'm looking around. And the first thing I noticed that it looked a lot brighter. While on the stretcher I'm able to see wallpaper and pictures on the walls. I even saw a movie theater, as I'm rolled into Unit A room 143. Once inside of the room and after being placed onto a very small bed. I'm looking around and the room looks like a bedroom. When Marie came in, I mentioned to her that the bed was too small. 'I'll let them know Sergio', as she leaves the room. Once she returned 'I told the nurse and she said they'll order you a longer bed, but it will take a couple of days.

After a few days with having the new bed. 'I feel a lot better leaving you here Sergio compared to that other nursing home'. 'This one does seem to be better Marie, so thank you'. 'You're welcome but please remember what I told you that no nursing home is ever perfect', as she kissed me on the forehead and leaves. I'm just lying there feeling really depressed and discouraged about my situation. With tears in my eyes, as I'm wondering why me as I cried myself to sleep.

The following morning as I opened my eyes. I'm trying to think of something or anything that I may have done to deserve this, but I wasn't able to think of anything. Now I've done many things in my life that I'm not proud of, as I'm sure that we all have. But nothing I could think of that would garner something like this. And after laying there for hours feeling sorry for myself. I realized that I had to do something. If I wanted to change my situation for the better I had to do something because I don't want to live the rest of my life like this as a quadriplegic in a nursing home. I was feeling hopeless at first. I'm a total quadriplegic that's bed ridding. While I'm learning to depending on someone else to do everything.

A CENA would have to come into my room every day to feed me breakfast lunch and dinner. I would have to wait for a CENA or a nurse to come into my room. Then I would have to ask them for some water, as they would have to go get a plastic cup. Then sit me up in the bed and place a straw into my mouth for me to drink. While living that way I became really frustrating. I found myself multiple times questioning God as I'm asking why let me survive only to live like this, but knowing God there must be a purpose for my life that I haven't completed yet, so I had to learn how to fight my battle physically spiritually and emotionally. Now please know I am truly blessed to be alive. And I'm very grateful to see, speak and love my children again, but I'm also tired of living as a quadriplegic.

After a few days of being in the new nursing home. The CENA'S started coming into my room asking about taken a shower or a bed bath. I wasn't used to that and I knew that it would be very painful to be touched, and let alone to be washed, so I kept saying 'no thank you'. Also, I was very uncomfortable with being undressed as a stranger would bath me, but after a few days. I was starting to smell, so I would ask Marie to wash me. And while she was bathing me she would always say 'you really need to get a shower because you have a lot of dead skin all over your body and it's turning yellow', as she held up a large chunk of dead yellow skin. 'But a shower is really going to hurt Marie'. 'It may at first but that's something that you really must do Sergio'.

After a few days of getting several painful, and embarrassing bed baths from the CENAS. I started thinking about what Marie said, so when she came to visit with me, I told her 'I've been getting bed baths because I didn't want to keep asking you to bath me'. 'That's great Sergio, but you need a shower to get that dead skin off of you'. 'Those bed baths were painful enough I don't know about taken a shower'. 'What if I helped them give you a shower would you take one then?' "I'm not sure Marie it's going to hurt even more'. 'One of the reasons that it hurts so much is because of the dead skin'. As I'm thinking about what she had said. 'I'll tell you what the next time you come up I'll take a very painful shower', as I begin to laugh. 'Okay then good it's a date, so the next time that I'm up here', as she leaves.

A few days later after talking with Marie for a while, she asked 'so are you ready'? 'Ready for what'? 'Your shower you said next time I'm up here, so I'm here to help'. 'No, I'm not ready but I'll do it anyway', as Marie hit my call light. When the CENA came in 'he would like to get a shower please and I'm going to help'. 'Okay I'll be right back with the shower bed and Hoyer', as she leaves. 'You know I'm going to regret this right?' 'You'll be fine I'll take care of you okay'

Chapter 90 A Portable Fridge

After ten minutes, my CENA returned, as I'm instructed on what to do. After being rolled onto my side as she placed the Blue Hoyer Pad under me. Then she brought over the Hoyer and connected the Pad to the Hoyer. I'm already in much pain from being rolled over. Then she brought the shower bed over near the foot of my bed and she asked, 'so are you ready?' 'No, I'm not but go ahead', as she pressed the remote to the Hoyer and I'm slowly lifted out of bed. Then she placed me onto the shower bed. With tears in my eyes as a flat sheet was placed on top of me. My CENA started pushing the shower bed down the hall and into the shower room.

Once in the shower room, my CENA took the Pad from up under me and my gown as I'm lying there embarrassed. Then Marie said, 'you'll be fine Sergio', as they begin to shower me. With tears running down my face. As I'm feeling as if I'm being scraped alive. 'Are you okay Sergio?' 'No, I'm not y'all killing me'! 'I'm almost done', as they continued. Then after almost an hour there done. Then I'm rolled back into my room.

Once placed back into my bed and my face is wet from tears. 'I'm sorry about that Sergio but it had to be done. And you still have some dead skin on you'. 'O well, it will be there because I'm not going through that shit again'. But I did, as I started getting showers once a week without Marie. And I noticed the more showers I took the less it seemed to hurt.

I've had to share a room with several residents since being here. My first roommate was a much older African American Man. That told me he had a stroke and was on a portable feeding tube. I was in bed one which is near the bathroom, so whenever he would walk to the bathroom in the middle of the night. He would wake me up. And I would always get a strong whiff of odor but not from the bathroom, but from him. He never showered or bathed, so he smelled horrible. And within a week, the whole room would smell, like him. He wore the same clothes for several weeks at a time. Without washing so that just added to the horrific odor. I'm unable to avoid smelling him, so I had to just lay there and gage.

He's not supposed to eat or drink, but he would steal milk and food off of the breakfast and lunch carts every day. And after several weeks of complaining to Marie about the food that I'm being feed not having any kind of flavor. And she said 'that's probably because of the people here can't have salt or whatever. I could bring you up some food but only whenever I visit'. Then on her next visit, she walked into my room with a small red cooler. 'I couldn't get that much into my cooler', as she took out what she brought and started feeding me. 'I need to get you a portable fridge, so I won't have to keep bringing food in my little cooler'.

And after a few weeks of bringing me food. I seen Marie come into my room pushing a nursing home Dolly with a big box that had a portable fridge inside. Once, she opened and set up the fridge then she put It onto my nightstand. 'Now I can bring you more food that you can keep in your fridge. Also, I don't have to remember to bring you food in my cooler anymore'.

About a week after having my fridge. My roommate got up to go to the bathroom one night. And I woke up and I looked at the clock on the wall and it's 4 am. Then I saw that he hadn't gone into the bathroom, but he had his hand on my fridge, so when I saw that, I shouted, 'what the hell are you doing?' 'Nothing', as he walked back to his side of the room. And we started fusing and cursing at one another for several hours through the curtain that divided the room until I fell back asleep.

The next day when Marie came to visit, I told her about what happened. And she said 'but doesn't he have a feeding tube?' 'Yes, he does, but he steals food and milk from the carts every day'. 'You should ask about getting a padlock put on your fridge'

Chapter 91 The Gym

The next day I asked and got a padlock put onto my fridge. And after months of dealing with the smell and his light being on all night. The nursing home moved him into a different Unit in the nursing home. And I had that room to myself for about a week. Then another resident was placed into that room. And after about a month, he left, and I had the room to myself again. But only for two weeks, as another resident was placed into the room. And this person that was placed into the room couldn't walk. So, I didn't have to worry about my fridge.

I would have a wound nurse come into do my treatment every day. At first, I was giving about twelve different narcotics a day. And now I take none; I also have a catheter. That must be changed every thirty days. Now that's painful to be changed and especially as a quadriplegic. Now for those that may not know what a catheter is. It's a long skinny tube that's connected to a deflated balloon. That's inserted into your bladder and at the end of that tube is a foley bag that collects the urine. The nurse would insert the catheter into my bladder through my penis. Once the catheter is in the bladder. The nurse would inject saline into the balloon through the top of the catheter.

And after several months of being depressed about my situation. I felt that I had to do something else other than just pray. So I tried to move. At first, maybe once or twice an hour. Then several times an hour for many months. Then one early morning while I was trying to move my arm. I was shocked when I move my right arm just a little. And I cried out of happiness. And once that happens, I became even more determined and motivated to keep trying to move. And within seven months of being quadriplegic. I'm able to move everything but no one knew.

So every day I had a routine of different exercises that I would perform. They were exercise that I felt was helping me to increase my mobility. Once I learned how to change my thoughts. My body seemed to changed as well. I had to learn how to use my anger about my situation to help fuel my determination.

I had a restorative therapist that would come into my room three times a week. And she would do some range of motion on my hands and legs before putting on my splints. To help my fingers binned and my feet sit upright. That I would wear on my feet and hands for several hours.

After several months of being able to move. I decided that I would show Marie. So the next time that she came to visit, I told her, 'I have a surprise for you' 'for me Sergio?' 'Yes', as I began moving my arms and legs and she looked amazed as she started crying. I told her, 'don't start crying you're going to make me cry. And I told her 'I've been moving every day for several months now and it's paying off'. 'Have you shown anyone this Sergio?' 'No, just you but I don't want anyone to know yet. I will just keep doing what I've been doing and I'm hoping that my movement gets a lot better'.

Now it's October of 2011 and I'm able to move everything. And once Marie came up, she convinced me to let her tell the nurses. So I could begin physical therapy. Once she told my nurse, a few of the nurses walked into my room with Marie. And she said, 'show them Sergio', as I started lifting both of my legs off of my bed. And I moved both of my arms up and down. And one nurse said, 'your defiantly moving', as they looked on in amazement. Then my nurse said, 'we need to notify therapy about your progress', as they leave.

The next day someone from physical therapy came into my room. And said, 'I heard that you could move now'. 'Yes, I can'. 'So let me see', as I began to move, he said 'you're definitely moving, so I need to get you into the gym. But you're going to need a wheelchair, so I'll work on that now', as he leaves. After a week I got a wheelchair. And I'm told 'you'll be coming into the gym soon'.

Now it's November and I've been placed into a wheelchair several times and pushed into the therapy gym. The gym is a huge therapy room with several pieces of equipment. I got an hour of physical therapy four days a week. After my second week, I'm told 'we're going to stand you up inside of the parallel bars next week'. The next time Marie came up I told her 'there going to stand me up next week'. 'That's great Sergio I'm going to come up here to watch on my lunch break'.

The following week I'm brought into the gym as I sat there feeling rather nervous. Then about five minutes later, I saw Marie as there positioning me in between the bars. I saw about seven therapists that were huddled around the bars, as they are there to help assist me in standing. A therapist puts a gate belt around me then I'm given a countdown '1,2,3', as they helped me to stand. I was really nervous as I stood until I looked around. And I saw that everyone that was helping seemed to be pretty short and my nervousness just went away.

The following week I was stood up once but with a lot less help. And for the next several months, I only did the Omni bike and pulleys, as I became really frustrated with the lack of physical therapy. One morning while in the gym. The therapy manager told me I should qualify for a power chair. And she asked, 'would you want one?' 'Yes, I would but how much will it cost me?' 'If you qualify, your insurance will cover the cost'. 'Then I would like one, so how long will it take to know whether or not I qualified?' 'I'm thinking no more than three months, in fact, I'm going to fill out your paperwork right now' and she goes into the office.

Chapter 92 'Do You Want To Try It Out'

After more than three months while in the gym. I asked her, 'so what happened?' 'I don't know but I'm going to send your paperwork in again'. And after several more months while in the gym. I'm working with the manager of therapy. And as she's setting me up onto the Omni bike and I made a comment saying 'I couldn't wait to walk again'. And she looked and said, 'you'll never walk again Mr. McGee you have a spinal cord injury'. And I told her 'I don't know if I have a spinal injury or not, but I will walk again and you'll see', as she walked away. Once done with therapy, I'm pushed near the nurse station. Where I waited to be placed back into bed.

And once back into bed, I was so frustrated at what she said. That I decided that I had to do even more exercise on my own to get myself walking again. And at that time, my exercise routine took me about two hours, so I decided to double my workout. And the fact that she said that told me she had decided that I wouldn't walk again. So I found myself questioning myself anytime that I worked with her, and even if she thought that she should've never said that, so that instantly became even more fuel for my determination. Of wanting to show her and everyone else that didn't believe that I will walk again.

So after eleven months, I'm finally told that I've been approved. 'That's great but what took so long?' 'I really don't know but I just keep sending in your paperwork until you were approved'. I thanked her for being so persistent and I'm told 'you're welcome Sergio. Then I'm told 'the power chair company should be here soon to get your measurements'. And about a week later, a guy arrived to take my measurements for my power chair. He asked, 'how tall are you?' 'I'm 6/1' 'how much do you weight'? And I said at that time 'about 200 pounds. 'I'll be back up here next week with another power chair for you to practice in, as you learn to operate the chair'.

The following week he came into my room and brought in a power chair. I hit my call light and when my CENA came in. I asked to get dressed and placed into that chair, as I pointed at the power chair. Once dressed and placed into the chair. I'm told 'these controls are just like the ones on your chair', as I proceed to drive up and down the hallways. The guy shouted, 'you're a natural', as I rode that chair for about twenty minutes. Then I asked him to hit my call light. And when my CENA arrived, I asked 'if I could get back into my bed now please?' 'Sure ', as she leaves to go get a Hoyer. Then once in my bed I'm told 'I'll see you again when your chair is ready'. And I asked, 'when will that be?' 'The end of this month or the beginning of next month', as he leaves. And when Marie came to visit, I told her about being approved for a power chair. 'And that I've already test drove one also'.

'That's great Sergio, so when will you get the chair?' 'The guy told me by the end of the month'. 'Now you'll be able to go anywhere you want without having to ask to be pushed'. 'That's so true', as she visited for a little longer then leaves.

The next afternoon I hit my call light when I had a BM around 4 pm. At that time, I couldn't roll over, so I had to just lay in my BM. My CENA and my nurse came into my room around 9:40 pm. And I asked, 'what took so long?' And I'm given some BS excuse, as the CENA cleaned me up.

The next time when Marie came to visit. I told her about what happen, and she couldn't believe that but reminded me of what she told me at the hospital'. 'I know what you said. No nursing home will ever be perfect'.

Then on July 1st, 2012 the guy arrived with my new power chair. Then I'm asked, 'do you want to try it out'? 'Hell yeah,' and I hit my call light. After about thirty minutes I'm dressed and in my chair. And I drove up and down the hallway. And I'm told the chair weighs 315 pounds and I'm asked 'does the chair fit?' And I answered 'yes it does' and I'm told 'that's why I needed your measurements'. Then after several minutes, I hit my call light to get back into the bed. Once back into the bed, I'm told 'your all set Mr. McGee here's all the instructions and information about your chair'. Then I asked him, 'could you put that into my nightstand please?' After placing the brochures into my nightstand. I'm told 'if you have any problems with your chair just have them call me and I'll be back up' then he leaves.

The next day I'm excited to get into my chair, so I hit my call light to get dressed and into my chair. Once in my chair, I cruised the hallways for a few hours. Then I asked my CENA if I could get back into the bed now? The next morning, I had therapy and I hit my call light. And once dressed and in my power chair. I went into the gym and was told, 'your power chair sits up to high you need to be in your manual wheelchair'. I couldn't do the Omni bike, so I just did the pulleys and ankle weights. I was still exercising every day on my own plus therapy.

Then one day after my therapy section I'm told I'll no longer be able to come to the gym. And I asked, 'why is that?' I'm told 'you're being dropped from therapy for lack of showing progress'. Then I'm told 'we maybe able to pick you back up in a few months' and then I'm pushed near the nurse station. Where I waited to get back into bed.

Then once I got back into bed, I'm really frustrated and I'm thinking of how I am not showing enough progress. When I went from a total quadriplegic and now, I'm doing physical therapy. I went almost a year without any kind of therapy. I wasn't even being told when I maybe able to return to therapy again. I've had therapists tell me several times. How I'm really working hard but I'm not getting any therapy now. That didn't make much sense to me it's some BS there not trying to help me walk again. So now I need to do even more exercises on my own.

Then on October 3rd, 2012, I'm moved from my room in Unit A into a room in Unit D. But I'm not being told the reason for the move. And after a week of being in that new room. I asked one of the CENA'S 'what's going on I've seen several people being moved into this Unit'. And I'm told 'A Unit is being turned into a quick rehabilitation Unit and this Unit is now our long-term Unit,' and then she leaves. I'm lying in bed and I'm feeling even more frustrated. Because now I know they're looking at me as a long-term situation. I became so upset I started exercising even more.

Chapter 93 After Weeks Of Practice

After a few weeks, I had developed a new routine for exercising. I was doing 1500 crunches and 500 leg lifts on each leg. I also was doing 150 arm bends and 500 finger bends on each arm and hand. And at first, it took me about three or four hours to complete my exercise routine. But after a few months, I had dwindled that down to about thirty seven minutes. And after a few weeks, the CENA'S started getting me dressed and into a Jerry Chair. Now a Jerry Chair isn't a wheelchair. It's more like a recliner on wheels. I would be pushed near the nurse station. Where I would painfully sit and wait for several hours to be put back into bed.

And after almost a year, I'm told that I'll be receiving physical therapy again. Then after about a month therapy got me another wheelchair, and I waited to be evaluated. Once my evaluation was completed. And after a few days, I'm placed into a wheelchair and pushed into the gym. I'm not able to push myself because I've lost the grip on my hands. So I was back to getting one hour of therapy four days a week, but I'm only doing the Omni bike and pulleys. And after a few months, an Occupational Therapist started working with me on my hands. I was doing different exercises that were to help me bend my fingers more, and help me with my grip. Then all the nurses and CENAS and residents that lived and worked in A Unit. We're transferred to D Unit and my room was 329 bed 2 which was near the window.

The room was like my old room, but it seemed to be really tight. I had my fridge on my nightstand again. And whenever anyone would visit, they would have to get a chair and set it at the foot of my bed. I had many problems while in that room and not just with my multiple roommates.

Then finally a telephone was placed into my room. But I couldn't use the telephone. So after weeks of practicing on how to use the telephone. I'm now able to use the telephone and my first call was to Marie. Because I knew her telephone number by heart. And when she answered the telephone, she asked, 'who did you have to call me this time'? Because I would have CENA'S call her for me and they would place the telephone up to my ear. So when I told her 'I called you on my own' and I started laughing. 'That's great so how did you learn to use the telephone?' 'I've been practicing for a few weeks now, so I decided to call you'. And we talked for a while then I called her mother and then mine. I eventually had a problem with every roommate that I had in that room. And after years of asking for a private room. Only to be told there isn't one available and that my insurance doesn't pay enough for a private room.

Then in September of 2013, I'm moved into a private room, that's around the corner from my old room, but still in D Unit. Once my bed was inflated and all my things were brought into the room. I'm placed into my bed and as I looked around the room. And the room seemed to be a lot wider and a little larger. My mother along with Marie's mother, had gotten me some three draw plastic storage containers. That was placed into my room and Marie had placed some of my clothes into the storage containers. Because over the years, I had accumulated a lot of clothes. And there wasn't enough room in just my closet.

Then shortly after I started receiving telephone calls from a few members of my family. I'm assuming that my mother gave them my number. And I thought that was cool that they called but I have family that lives out of state. That has visited me more than some of my family that lives near where I'm at in Michigan. And that bothered me for many years. I've done a lot for many in my family, and to not even get a call or a visit still bothers me some.

Then one day towards the end of September in 2013. I received a telephone call from my cousin Tina, that lives in Atlanta Georgia. And she's one of my family members that would visit me while she was in Michigan. And as we're talking, I told her about how it was bothering me that many members of our family hadn't visited or even called. 'They have their lives Sergio' 'and I agreed but after being here for several years. And they can't even find the time to visit or even call'. 'I don't know why they haven't visited or called, but you can't worry about that. You only need to worry about getting yourself better, so you can get out of that nursing home'. 'Your right I just don't understand why'. 'And you may never understand Sergio, but enough about that how are you doing'? 'I'll be okay I'm just wanting out of this nursing home and to become independent again'. 'You will Sergio'. 'I know I will. It's just taken a lot longer then I hoped'. 'Other than therapy what else do you do?' 'Not much really other than watching television and there's nothing on most of the time. I wish I had a laptop computer'. 'I thought you had one'. 'No, I don't' as we talked about something else. Then while we're talking, she interrupted me and said, 'I just bought you an iPad online'. 'You don't have to do that', 'but I already did, so what city dose your friend Marie live in?' 'Westland Michigan'. 'Okay, just have her pick it up at the Best Buy store in Westland'. I thanked her again and once off the telephone.

I called Marie and I told her what just happen. 'That's great Sergio I'll pick it up for you'. And after a week, Marie brought up my iPad. 'I also bought you a keyboard a screen protector and got you some insurance. That way if something happens or it gets damaged. Also, I put some apps on there for you already like Netflix, ESPN, Facebook, the Bible and others'. Once I went to use my iPad, I started having problems getting online. I noticed that the Wi-Fi signal in my room wasn't very strong. 'I'll get you something to help boost your signal'. And after a few weeks, Marie had gotten something to help boost my Wi-Fi signal and once she plugged it into an outlet. I was able to get online with no problems.

Now it's January 2014 when I'm informed that I've been dropped from therapy again.

Chapter 94 'Let's Do It Again'

Once Marie came in, I told her that I had been dropped from physical therapy again. 'That's some bullshit Sergio', 'I agree' no one in therapy works harder than me. I've seen people in therapy refusing to do therapy and some even asleep while on the Omni bike. I once even told a therapist 'there asleep'. He looked and said, 'it's okay I'll wake them up when their time is done'. Meanwhile, I'm never refusing and busting my ass every day and I'm still dropped. Then I found out that it's all about the money because you're only allowed so much money per year through your insurance. And that determines whether or not you get therapy. Not the lack of showing progress but meanwhile, the therapist gets paid regardless if you show progress or not. And I'm whiling to bet you if they only got paid only based on the progress of the person they're working with. I'm sure that everyone would be showing much more progress. I'm starting to feel they don't want me to walk again. They rather keep me in this nursing home forever and continue to get paid from my insurance. But that's not going to happen. I will walk on my own even if no one in this nursing home believes me.

I would get into my power chair a couple of days a week. I just wanted to get out of my room. All though I never socialized with the residents. Other than being polite and speaking because most people that are here are several decades older than me. And, I feel like everyone that I've seen in therapy seemed to have just given up. They're not even trying to better themselves to get out of this nursing home. It's almost as if they enjoy being waited on hand and foot.

Now it's the middle of March 2014 when a new physical therapist came into my room. And he introduced himself and told me he was there to evaluate me for therapy. Once done bending my arms and legs. I'm told, 'I think that you can walk Mr. McGee'. 'I've been saying that for a while now!' Then I asked him, 'can I show you a video of me sitting on the side of my bed with no help?' 'Sure, so I played the video for him on my iPad. After watching my video I'm told 'I would like to see you do that now', so I sat on the side of my bed. Then after helping me get my legs back into the bed. I'm told, 'I would like for you to come down to the gym,' and I asked, 'when tomorrow?' 'No today now'. Then I'm told 'I'll go get you a wheelchair 'and he leaves.

So, I hit my call light for my CENA and once she came in, I asked her to help get me dressed. And once the therapist returned with a wheelchair. I was already dressed with the Hoyer Pad under me. Then I'm placed into the wheelchair and pushed into the gym.

Once in the gym, he begins to stretch me out some. Then I was placed between the parallel bars and he helped me to stand up three times. Once done, I'm told 'I'll see you tomorrow', as I'm pushed out of the gym.

Once back into bed, I called Marie and told her about what happened. That's great, Sergio, so you're getting physical therapy again?' 'He said I'll see you tomorrow so yeah, I believe I am'. I went into the gym four days in a roll with my new therapist Mr. Nawab. And he stood me up thirteen times in those four days. And I told him, 'you know you've stood me up more in four days. Then I've been stood up in over three years. 'I don't know why that is, but I'll be working with now, so I'll see you next week', as I'm taken near the nurse station.

Once in bed and when Marie came in, I told her about my new therapist and how I've stood up more in four days. Then I had in over three years. 'That's good so you finally got someone that's working with you the way that you need!' And I told her what I appreciated about working with him. He speaks to me and with me direct. He seems to believe in me almost as much as I believe in myself. I was only posted to get one hour of physical therapy time. But there were many times that he would work with me a little longer. Then he noticed that whenever I would take steps inside of the parallel bars, my toes would drag. So he found a brace that would help my toes not drag. The black metal brace that went inside of my gym shoe. The part of the brace that went inside of my shoe was a metal footprint. And the part that was under my toes was lifted and the brace also had velcro straps that would be wrapped around my calf. 'I found this brace in a storage room, so I'll order you another now that I know it works'. After a few weeks, the other brace had arrived. And every time before I would stand. He would place the braces inside of my gym shoes. Then he would trap the velcro around my cafes. And after several weeks of just standing between the bars. I'm told 'the next time that we stand, I want you to take some steps.

And the first time that I stood, I took three steps and sat back down. Then he said, 'let's do it again,' and this time he stood in front of me. With his gate belt wrapped around my waist. Then he placed his foot between mine and I took five steps. Then he said, 'I noticed that your right leg swings towards your left leg. So that's why I placed my foot between yours'. He explained, 'because you haven't walked in a while. Your muscles are overcompensating. Then he said, 'I would like to start getting you into your wheelchair with a sit to stand machine instead of the Hoyer. That way I can get you onto the workout mat and do even more therapy-related things with you'.

The following week once in the gym. He had a sit to stand machine and Pad. 'I want to try this out and see if it works, so lean forward', as he placed the Pad behind and under me. Then he hooked the sit to stand to the Pad and said, 'here we go', as I'm lifted up into a standing position. Once I'm standing, he said 'its works' then he asked, 'how does it feel'? 'It's better than a Hoyer but this Pad feels too small', as I'm lowered back into the wheelchair. 'I'll just have to order you a much larger Pad because you're a pretty tall guy. But at least I know that you can get into a wheelchair with a sit to stand now'.

Chapter 95 'I Want To Thank You'

After several weeks. My special ordered sit to stand pad arrived. The CENA got me into my wheelchair with the sit to stand. Then the CENA brought me into the gym and went back to bring the sit to stand machine into the gym. While in the gym on some days, I would stand and take steps between the parallel bars. And on other days, he would place me onto the mat, and he would do different type of stretches and exercises.

A few times he even came into my room. Were we looked on YouTube for other exercises I could also do in therapy. We started doing this one exercise where I'm placed onto the mat. And he would put an armed chair next to the mat. Then I would put my elbows into the chair. And I would work my way up to the top of the chair. And once I had reached the top of the chair. I was in a somewhat standing position. While doing that exercise was very difficult at first, but the more I did it the better I became. After a week of trying to do that exercise. I was able to do it every time without a problem.

Then I started getting urinary tract infections. And I knew with having a catheter I'm subject to getting them. But whenever I would take antibiotics to get rid of it. The next month or so, I would get another one. I had gotten a UTI so bad I literally had puss and blood coming out of the bottom of my testicle sack. After a few weeks, I ended up being sent to Oakwood Hospital. While in the hospital, a bullet from when I got shot in 1990 appeared on top of my skin. So my doctor from the nursing home came up to the hospital and removed the bullet. I asked to keep the bullet and when Marie came to visit. I told her about the bullet, and I gave her the bullet to keep for me. And even before I was sent to the hospital. I still would go to therapy as I was bleeding and very sore. With a temperature over a hundred degrees. Because my attitude was no matter how I feel sick or whatever. I'm going to therapy if I'm physically able. The next day after leaving the hospital. I went into the gym and Mr. Nawab looked and said, 'I heard that you were in the hospital. 'I was but I'm back so let's get to work'.

After several weeks of therapy. I'm now taken seventeen steps forward and sixteen backward inside of the parallel bars. We had developed a routine for my therapy. On certain days I would stand and take steps. And on other days, I would do the standing frame or be stretched out and exercise on the mat. The standing frame is a contraption that can stand you up from a wheelchair. I would roll up between the standing frame. And the therapist would remove the armrest on the wheelchair. Then my therapist would place a harness around my bottom and lower back. Then the therapist would connect the harness to the standing frame.

Once done, the therapist would hit the remote and I'm slowly lifted into a standing position. I was told 'for every thirty seconds that you stand, your body naturally stretches you out better than I ever could'.

After a few days, I started asking him to loosen the harness and I began doing squats. Then I'm told 'that's really good for you to do Sergio because it will help strengthen your quad muscles in your legs'. So, whenever I would do the standing frame, I would ask for the harness to be loosened so I could do my squats. And he would tell me 'you're really working hard every time that your down here your t-shirt is always soaked'. 'I'm going to walk again so I'm going to do whatever I can to make that happen. No matter how hard it maybe to achieve my goal, I'm going to do it'. 'I believe you will because you can't fake sweet and you're always soaked in sweet'.

Then after several months of working with Mr. Nawab. I'm told 'after my vacation, I will no longer be working here'. 'Why?' 'There's another nursing home that's five minutes from my house, so I'll be working there when I get back. But I just wanted you to know that it's been a pleasure working with you. I wish everyone that I've worked with had your attitude about working because that would make my job a lot easier'. 'I just want to thank you for believing in me when no one else at this nursing home did'. 'The week before I leave, I'm going to have another therapist work with us, so they'll know what to do. But I already know that you'll let them know also'. And during his last week, he had another therapist working with us. Then I started noticing that I was having a double vision while watching television. I eventually told Marie about it and she asked, 'so long have you been experiencing this?' 'A few weeks', 'so why are you just now saying something?' 'I thought that it might go away'.

Chapter 96 'I Had To Fuse'

Marie called my social worker at the nursing home. And they scheduled me an appointment to visit with an eye doctor at the nursing home. After a few weeks, I got into my power chair and went to my eye opponent in a big conference room where the doctor was set up. And once my exam was complete. I'm told that I have cataracts in both eyes. And that's the reason behind the double vision'. He wrote down recommendations of who I should go see to get that taken care of. Then he handed me that paper and some eye drops.

Once I went back to my unit, I asked my nurse to make a copy of the paperwork and I kept the original. Once back in my bed, I called Marie and told her about my exam. 'He said I need cataract surgery on both eyes. And when she came up, I showed her the paper of the recommendations and she picked a place.

Then a few weeks later when transportation arrived. I left for my appointment. Where I meet with a cataract specialist, that's in Dearborn, Michigan. After completing my exam, I'm told, 'you need cataract surgery on both eyes. And I will do one eye at a time starting with your right eye first because it's the worse', as he scheduled my surgery for December 4th, 2014. Then on December 4th at 5:30 am transportation arrived with a stretcher. Once on the stretcher, I'm taken to Heritage Hospital in Taylor, Michigan. I'm taken into a room and transferred from the stretcher onto a bed. Where I had a nurse come into put an IV into my arm. Then I'm given several eyes drops into my right eye. And around 12 pm, I'm taking into an operating room. Where the specialist / surgeon performed my surgery as I'm lying there talking with him. Then after about fifteen minutes, he's done, and I'm taken back into the same room. With a clear patch over my right eye. Then I'm given three bottles of eye drops. And I'm told to keep that patch on my eye for ten days. And to get each eye drop three times a day, but fifteen minutes apart until every bottle is emptied. 'And I'll do your other eye next month,' and I leave.

Once back at the nursing home. I explained to my nurse what the doctor told me. And I handed the nurse the kit I was given. The kit was a small black bag with several clear patches. And a roll of tape and some large (Blue Blocker) sunglasses. And for the next ten days, I wore that patch over my eye. And nurses would come into my room three times a day putting those eye drops into my eye. I even went to the gym the next day with the patch and sunglasses. After about thirty days, I'm all out of the eye drops.

And now it's the end of November 2014 and I'm working with my new therapist Mr. Malone. He's not Mr. Nawab but he's not bad. We worked together and I'm doing most of the things that I was doing. And after several weeks of doing the same things. I'm told 'let's try using the walker in between the bars. 'Okay but I have my own walker in my room,' and he leaves. When he returned with my walker, he placed it in between the bars. And I asked, 'so how are we going to do this?' 'I think I'll place the walker in front of you. Then I'll stand behind the walker. And once I help you to stand, you'll just grab the walker and then the bars. 'I'm not sure about this but alright', as he helped me to stand. And I tried to grab the walker but I couldn't, so I tried again. And that time I grabbed the walker and I took two steps.

Then he said, 'let's try the walker outside of the bars'. 'I've never tried that but okay', as I rolled myself with my sticky football gloves on in my wheelchair near the car in the gym. He placed the walker in front of me and placed his gate belt around my stomach. Then he asked, 'are you ready'? 'No, I'm not but I'm going to try'. 'Okay, here we go 1,2,3', as he helped me to stand. And once up I'm holding onto the walker. And I took four steps and sat back down and laughed. I couldn't believe what I had just done, and my therapy time was up. And I'm told 'that's what we're going to do from now on just use your walker outside of the bars'.

The next time in the gym I'm doing the standing frame. And I stood up three times at four minutes each time. And I did my fifty squats each time I stood. I also did the bars where I stood up three times and I took seventeen steps forward and fifteen steps backward. Every day that I would walk with my walker. I always took more steps. I went from only taken four steps in the beginning to taken over fifty steps.

One day I brought my iPad into the gym. Because I wanted to document my progress. After asking if I could videotape myself. I'm told that I can, if it's only me on videotape and I agreed. I asked the therapist to place my iPad on the table and point it towards me, as I did the bars. Then a therapist held my iPad and I took over twenty steps with my walker.

It's now January 14th, 2015 and I'm in the gym. I would always walk with my walker first while my legs were still fresh. I would have one therapist behind me to push my wheelchair. And my therapist standing in front of me. He would place his gate belt around my waist. Then once I'm helped up, I would grab the walker and I would begin to take steps. Now before that session I was told by the new therapy manager. 'It's not about the number of steps that you take, but the quality of the steps. So, with that in mind, I'm trying to stand up straighter and with less help from my therapist, I felt. So, I took about ten steps and as I went to sit back into my wheelchair. I felt and heard a loud pop and I grabbed my left knee. Then I asked, 'did you hear that?' Mr. Malone 'no hear what?' 'That loud pop and my left knee really hurt. I can't even lift my leg onto the leg rest'. Then I'm asked, 'do you think it's broke?' 'I'm not sure it doesn't feel as bad as my other leg felt when it was broke'. Then he rubbed on my leg to see if it felt broken. 'I can't tell if it's broken, but it doesn't feel broken. We're not going to do the parallel bars. I'll just put you on the pulleys and standing frame. I did the pulleys without any problem other than the pain. Then I'm put onto the standing frame and my pain rapidly increased. I usually would do fifty squats, but it hurt so bad that I only did about twenty-eight painfully squats. And I told him 'take me off it hurts to much'. Once in my wheelchair, I'm told, 'I'm going to let your nurse know about your leg,' and I rolled myself out of the gym.

Now that happen at around 10:30 am and I'm put back into bed after 11 am. My nurse came in an asked 'what happens?' After explaining, I'm told 'I'll order some X-rays on your leg'? Then I asked, 'how long will that take?' 'A couple of hours' and he leaves. Then around 4 pm, a male X-ray tech came into my room. After taking a few painful X-rays I asked him, 'is it broke?' 'I'm not supposed to tell you your nurse is, but yes, it's broke,' and he leaves. I waited a while to see if I'll be sent to the hospital. Then when Marie called, I explained what happen and how I've been waiting. Then around 6:30 pm when Marie came into visit me after work. She said 'I can't believe they haven't sent you to the hospital yet for something that happens this morning', as she leaves out of my room. After about twenty minutes, she returned. 'I had to fuse, but they're finally going to send you out'.

Chapter 97 'What's That'?

Then around 7:30 pm transportation arrived, and I'm taken to Oakwood Hospital in Dearborn Michigan. Once at the hospital on a stretcher in the hallway. As I'm waiting with Marie for a room to become available. Then after about three hours, I told Marie to just go home. 'Are you sure?' 'Yeah, I'll be okay'. Once she left, I watched several people that got there after me get a room.

Then around 4 am I'm finally taken back into a room. Then shortly after I'm taken for a CAT SCAN. Once done, I'm taken to a private room around 5:30 am. Once in the bed a nurse came into the room. And I'm asked several questions and as I'm answering her questions. She said, 'I see here, as she pointed towards her computer. That you have a history of Osteoporosis'. 'What is that?' This is the first time that I've heard of that. And the fact that you said history tells me this has been known'. 'I'm just telling you what I see here. You broke your other leg last year right?' 'I did but I wasn't told that last year'. 'Also, you can't eat or drink anything for twenty five hours'. 'Why is that?' 'The doctor may need to perform surgery on your broken Femur Bone,' and she leaves. And I eventually fall asleep.

The next afternoon I'm told 'you can eat and drink now and you won't need to have surgery because your fracture is near your knee cap. You don't even need a cast it will be healed in about six to eight weeks on its own'. Then I asked, 'can I get a stabilizer?' 'Sure, but you don't need it', as I'm given a stabilizer. I was hospitalized from Friday evening until Tuesday afternoon. While there, I received a few visits from my daughter Marie and my cousin Monica.

Once back at the nursing home and placed back into my bed. I'm lying there in such pain and frustration. Then after an hour or so, Marie walked into my room. 'How are you feeling?' 'I'm frustrated and I'm in pain and my leg itches'. 'You want me to wash your leg and put some powder on it?' 'Yeah, if you think that will help'. 'I'll be right back,' and she leaves to get a face rag. When she returned, she gingerly removed the stabilizer. Then wash and powdered my leg. Once done, I'm asked, 'how does that feel now?' 'It doesn't itch so thank you but it still hurts.

'I'm sorry I can't fix that'. And we started talking for a while then she leaves.

After a few days, I was still trying to exercise. But I was bedridden so I had gained some weight. I had mentioned to Marie several times that I wanted to become a vegetarian. But she did most of my cooking at that time, and whatever she would cook, I would get brought to me, but she wasn't ready. So, I just stopped asking. It was near the end of the month, so I called my mother because she would bring me food up once a month. And I told her, 'I don't want any more meat when you bring me up some food please. I'm a vegetarian now, so no meat please'

Chapter 98 Once I Changed My Thoughts

A few days after the first of the month. My youngest brother Micheal brought our mother up to visit, and to bring me some food. After putting the food away into my fridge. She did some leg bending exercises with me and once done. We talked for a while and they left.

I've been waking up around 2 am every morning for several years now. We're I would do several different exercises, then I would have a BM. Then after being cleaned up, and on days that I had therapy. I would ask the midnight CENA to help me get dressed. Then after several hours, I would hit my call light to get into my wheelchair before 7 am. I was told to be in front of the gym and ready to go at 8 am. But the first couple of times the midnight CENA didn't come into my room early enough, so I was late. So, I started hitting my call light even earlier. That way the CENA would have enough time to get me into my wheelchair and I would be in front of the gym at 8 am. I wanted to strengthen my arms so whenever I would walk either between the parallel bars or my walkers. I'll have the upper body strength that's needed to hold myself up, and also, I wanted to lose some weight. So once in my manual wheelchair. I started doing five laps up and down the hallways before therapy. And be in front of the gym by 8 am. And every week I would add a few more laps until I got up to ninety laps. Then after several months of asking to do the pulleys while in the gym. I'm told that I now get thirty minutes instead of fifteen minutes. And that's fifteen minutes for the omni bike and fifteen minutes for the pulleys. The weight on the pulleys wasn't 110 lbs. as it was before. It was set at only 35 lbs., so I would do ten sets of twenty five reps.

Then after several months of being told to be in front of the gym at 8 am. Now I'm being told to be ready at 7 am. And I felt the only reason for that time change was because they didn't think that I would make it, but to their surprise. I would just hit my call light even earlier and after doing my laps. I would still be in front of the gym at 7 am. I feel and felt they rather I stayed in the wheelchair. And not complain about not getting physical therapy, but that's not going to happen.

While doing my laps in the hallways. I would have staff members and even family members of residents stop me and say 'you're the only one that I see out here excising most days. 'Yeah, I know it's unfortunate but I will walk again, so I have to put in the hard work today for the miracle that may come tomorrow'. 'That's so true and I believe that you will walk again. Because you seem very determined'.I found it really strange how strangers can see something. That many of the therapists never seemed to acknowledge. I've learned that many may just not want to believe. And only until you do it and even then, some still won't believe. And that's fine with me because that just adds more fuel to my determination. You must want to do whatever it is for yourself and not others. One of the many things that I've learned from this life-altering experience. Once I changed my thoughts on how I looked at my situation. And I had more positive thoughts. My body began to changed for the better. Then on October 29th, 2015, my wound finally healed. And I believe that happen from changing my thoughts and my diet.

Now its 2016 and I never would've thought. That I would've been in here this long, but I just have to play the cards that I've been dealt. And continue doing the hard work that I've been doing and keep praying. Until I'm able to do the things that I once did, but until then. I'll just keep praising my God because I know without him, none of this would ever be possible. And I know that he doesn't put anything on you that you can't handle. So, in the meantime, I'll just keep on working very hard to get better, as I continue worshipping him. Until I'm out of here again and walking!

The End?

A Final Thought

This is a glimpse or clip note into my life story. I could've wrote several books to include everything, but this is a accurate look into my life from my perspective. I may write another book to document my progress and update those that are interested in my story because my story isn't done, as my struggle continues.

The End?

Stay #Blessed

Acknowledgments

To my three wonderful children. Cordial, Denzel and Nichole for being an inspiration in writing my life story. My hope is by reading, you will get a better understanding of who I am and why I am how I am. To my two beautiful grandchildren, you are the future. I'm looking forward to being involved in how you become great people. To my mother Louise we haven't always had the best of relationship, but it's a lot better now I love you. To my father, Leo, that wasn't always in my life, but I'm thankful for the time we shared rest in power. To my very large family on both sides I love you all. To my other family the Gunters that have been a blessing in my life since being in a nursing home I love you all. To Allene a very wonderful person that I will be forever thankful to have the pleasure of calling you a friend I love you. To Novi Providence Hospital there doctors nurses CENAS and house keepers. The nursing homes, nurses, doctors and CENA'S and physical therapist and house keepers. And everyone that has and is praying for me I am proof of the power of prayer. To those that gave me words of encouragement in person and online. To those that donated an shared my crowdfunding link. To my family and friends that visit me at the nursing homes. You guys will never know how much that really meant. I want to say thank you again.

Stay #Blessed

My Request

If you enjoyed reading #Blessed. Please leave a book review wherever you purchase my book. So others can enjoy my story as well. Thank you again for reading.

Stay #Blessed

Made in the USA
Monee, IL
25 April 2021